We
Really
Do
Need
To
Listen.

We ♥ Really Do Need To Listen.

Reuben Welch

impact
books

Nashville, Tennessee

OTHER BOOKS BY REUBEN WELCH

WE REALLY DO NEED EACH OTHER MO526 (HB)
MO798 (PB)

WHEN YOU RUN OUT OF FANTASTIC . . .
PERSEVERE MO511 (HB)

Library of Congress Catalogue Number 78-50098

Hardback	Paperback
ISBN 0-914850-84-9	ISBN 0-914850-69-5
MO522	MO544

First Edition

First Printing: May 1978
Second Printing: October 1978

Dedication

To My Mother
Sallie Harper Robinson Welch

Who has listened with her heart
and made me want to hear . . .

Contents

Introduction

DEAR FRIENDS, I HAVE SOME WORDS FOR YOU

(John 13:1-30)

Introduction

It is late Thursday night of Passion Week,
        the last week of Jesus' earthly life.
Tomorrow He will die.
        But on this night He is with the eleven
           in the quietness
                of the upper room.

Can you see that room?
        It has been so carefully prepared.
      Yet now, at the disciples' elbows, remain only
            the leftovers
                    of their meal.
          See the fragments of the broken bread?
              The dregs in the cup?
See there . . . at the end of the table
           the unfinished morsel
              which Judas couldn't stomach?
And there . . . in the corner
          a bowl of cloudy water
             and a very dirty towel?

Judas has already made his way into the night,
                              black
                              and
                              starless,
                    to betray his Lord.

Outside, the tide of hostility and animosity
                    is rising
                              to full hatred.
Tomorrow its waves will crash in on that small band of
    men
and almost destroy them.
But tonight they are together—
                    Jesus and His disciples—
                              and to them
                    He opens His heart . . .

This book was written in the belief that we—
          His present-day disciples,
          the twentieth-century body of believers—
                    really do need to listen
                              and
                              respond
          to the things Jesus shared that night.

The book is the substance of a series of Bible studies
    done in churches over a period of two years, during
    which there was, for me at least,
                    considerable
                    "creative
                              evolution."
Neither the Bible studies in the churches nor the
    chapters of this book adequately cover the themes
    found in the Scriptures.
(I sometimes get so involved in one idea
                    that there isn't time for another!
          The varying lengths of the chapters reflect this!)

Scripture passages are taken from the Revised Standard
Version of the Bible, and only the words of Jesus
appear in bold print.

Let us hear again some of the things
Jesus shared with His disciples
in that upper room
late on the eve of His death
as recorded for us in John 13:31 to 17:26.

The words of Jesus found in this beautiful section of
John's Gospel
have been called
"The Farewell Discourses"
or
"Jesus' Last Will and Testament to His Church."
They are a rich legacy.

I read somewhere once that in these discourses is
everything that is most precious to our Christian
heritage:

every gift,
every promise,
every commandment,
every warning,
every resource
that the living Christ ever gave to all who love Him in
sincerity and truth.

We are there, too!
Let's listen to the living Lord as He shares
the gifts,
the commandments,
the resources
we need for our Christian journey.

He speaks of His departure,
His going away.
He speaks of the coming of the Holy Spirit
and the quality of life to be lived within the fellowship
of His followers.
He speaks of His coming again.
He prays for the disciples—for their
holiness,
oneness,
love,
joy,
and for their sharing with Him in heaven the glory
of His Father.

It is important for us to know
that those eleven with Jesus that night represent
THE CHURCH.
They have shared the covenantal meal.
They have taken the bread of His broken body.
They have drunk the wine of His shed blood.
They have participated by faith in His given life
so soon
to be accomplished on Calvary.

Tomorrow they will be scattered.
Peter will deny Him.
Judas has already betrayed Him.
All the rest will run in fear.

They are weak and they are human—
BUT THEY ARE THE CHURCH!
To them, Jesus opens His heart.
For them, He goes to die!

AND WE ARE THE CHURCH—
        we who, by faith, have participated in that
           broken, given body and that poured-out
           blood—
        we who, by faith, now participate in the
           offered life of Christ
           through the ministry of the Holy Spirit.
      Even in our humanness and weakness,
      we are the Church—the Body of Christ.

I have the profound conviction that what the Lord Jesus
was saying to His Church then in
             preparation for His departure
He is saying to His Church now in the
             duration of His departure,
while He is yet present among us in the person of His
                            Spirit.

It is important, too, for us to know
      that the words of this farewell discourse were
        written
      some sixty years after that night of intimate
        fellowship
                        in the upper room.
                        They were written
after long years of profound meditation by the Apostle
   John
on the meaning of the "Christ event"—
      years during which he had experienced
                  deep
                    personal fellowship
with the risen, living Christ through the ministry of
   His Spirit.

I can only believe, then, that
>the right mental image for us
>as we read the discourses
>>is the risen Jesus in the midst of His Church.
>>>See the risen Jesus opening His heart
>>>to us who are His body, the Church!

From an historical point of view, the words of John
13—17 were spoken before the crucifixion.
>>But there is no way for
>the apostle not to see the Jesus of the Table
>>>as the risen Lord of the Church.

Mary Jo and I have been married more than thirty
years.
There is no way
>for me to think of her objectively
>>>as she was when I knew her as a single woman
>>>>in her late teens.

All my memories are affected by
>>the love and fellowship,
>>>the tears
>>>and joys
>>>and togetherness
>>of these intervening years.
>I believe that, in much the same way, the old apostle
was influenced
and affected
>by the years of intimate fellowship with his Lord.
The point is this:
>As we read these words, we need to hear them not
only
>>as words spoken
>>to the eleven
>>long ago in the upper room.
>They do not come to us as the words
>>>of a man now *dead*.

We desperately need to listen to the words
spoken by the *risen* Christ
to His Church today.
His words are
a living discourse
of One who lives
and whose words give *life*
to all who hear and believe.

The word *listen* is a significant word.
The basic concern I have is that Christians like you and
me do not take as seriously as we ought the words of Jesus.
We *hear* them.
We *read* them.
We *look* at them and have some vague
familiarity with them. But our lives are
actually
directed by them
far too little.
We need to hear, really hear,
the living Word of the living Christ
in the midst of His Church
in the power of His Spirit.

The theology of the whole Bible is, in fact, a theology of
the Word.
That is, God speaks the initiating
word and man responds in trustful love.
He speaks in creation,
in revelation,
in redemption.
He speaks through the long history of Israel in
preparation.

Then, in the fullness of time, God speaks to us
in His Son, Jesus,
the living Word,
who is an extension of Himself.
And His speaking is such that it demands a response.

In the Bible, then,

to listen
is to hear
is to respond
is to obey
is to believe!

When we say to our children,
"You listen to me!"
we really mean,
"Pay attention and obey!"

When Jesus said,
If any man hear my voice . . . (Revelation 3:20),
He was really saying,
**If any man listen to me, he must
respond
obey
believe.**
And, in the obedience of faith,
the way is opened for the sharing of His life and power.

Jesus has words for Christians
like you
and
me.
At least eight times in these Farewell Discourses,
He says:
**These things I have spoken to you.
(John 15:11)**

And in the great prayer of consecration,
He said: **I have given them the words
which thou gavest me.
(John 17:8)**

**You disciples—
you human-type people
with weakness and frailty
who yet share my life and live in this world
by my Spirit—
you who are living "between the times,"
I *have words for you!*
They are the words my Father gave me!**

WE REALLY DO NEED TO LISTEN!

Chapter One

DON'T TRY HARDER—TRUST MORE

(John 13:31 to 14:3)

Questions and interruptions; Funerals, failures, and unfaith; Jesus' going-away: its manner and meaning; Living life "between the times."

Chapter 1

Much of what Jesus said
to His friends in the upper room
that memorable night
was in response to their
QUESTIONS and INTERRUPTIONS.
John records four of them:
the first by Peter;
the second by Thomas;
the third by Philip;
the fourth by Judas, not Iscariot.

I've often been glad for those interruptions.
Some of the most beautiful and significant things
Jesus ever said were in response to them.
I sometimes wonder
if Jesus would have said
what He said if they hadn't
said what they said out of their
questioning, troubled hearts that night!
What is important is that *their* questions
are really *our* questions!
And that's why we need to listen!

Remember that the eleven are in the upper room with
Jesus on the night before His death.
We can almost feel with them the heaviness of
the atmosphere.
Profound changes are waiting just beyond the
locked door.
The disciples do not understand
their own sense of foreboding.
They cannot fathom the meaning of
the Supper they have shared.
They are experiencing both joy and
dread in the presence of their Lord.

Jesus begins to speak!
He tells of the glory implicit in
His coming death. Then, in words too weighty
to comprehend, He says:
Where I am going, you cannot come.
I think I can understand the
numb silence.
No questions.
No response.
Only silence.

And Jesus goes on to talk with them of
the old-new commandment:
Love one another.
But Peter doesn't hear. His head is
spinning with the impact of the words
he has just heard:
I am going,
I am going,
I am going.
Until, finally, the outburst:
"LORD, WHERE ARE YOU GOING?"

Let's look at Jesus' answer. It seems to me He rather led Peter to the answer by way of a detour, and I want to take that detour, too.

This is not precisely what I want to write about, except, as you know, the detours of a speaker or writer are sometimes better than the main road!

"LORD, WHERE ARE YOU GOING?"

Where I am going you cannot follow me now; but

you shall follow afterward. (John 13:36)

What a strange response!

Of course, Peter didn't give up. He persisted:

"Lord, why can't I follow you now? I will lay down my life for you!"

I think I would have said that, too.

Jesus answered:

Will you lay down your life for me? Truly, truly, I say to you, the cock will not crow, till you have denied me three times. (v. 38)

(Now, take out that big 14 at the chapter break and keep right on reading!)

Let not your hearts be troubled; believe in God, believe also in me. (14:1)

I am going.

Where are you going?

You can't follow me now.

Why? I will die for you!

No. You will, in fact, deny me.

Oh, no!

Oh, yes!

No way, Lord!

Yes, Peter, before morning. But let not your heart be troubled—believe! Believe in God, believe also in me.

Somehow, that last line doesn't go
with the others.
But that is indeed the line that follows the others.
And it's not an accident!
We are used to associating
that last line
with funerals, aren't we?
I suppose that beautiful passage
beginning with those words:
Let not your hearts be troubled . . .
is the classic scripture
for a Christian funeral.

I used it myself not long ago.
They are beautiful and healing words for
those who mourn.
But Jesus did not speak them in the context of
a *funeral;*
He spoke them in the context of
a *failure*.
So, thank God, they are also beautiful and
healing words
for those who fail!

Peter: I will die for you.
Jesus: **No, you will deny me before the
cockcrow of morning. But!
Let not your heart be troubled.**
Believe!

In full awareness of the reality of Peter's
impending failure,
Jesus called him and us
to renewed faith in the Father
and renewed faith in Himself!

Look at it this way!
 Did Peter want to fail?
 Of course not.
 Did he intend to fail?
 No.
 Did he think he would fail?
 No.
 Did he mean what he said when
  he said
   what he said?
 Yes.
 Did he intend to fulfill it?
 Yes.
 Was he sincere?
 Yes.

      BUT!

        Did he fail?
          Yes.
       Did he want to fail?
          No.
       Did he love Jesus?
         Oh, yes!
       Did he deny Jesus?
          Yes.
     Did he want to deny Him?
          No.
      Then why did he?

 Why, indeed?
I don't think I know the *answer,*
 but I sure do understand the *question!*
  God knows I've asked it enough times!
  Oh, yes, that's the question we ask ourselves
   in the times of our own failures.
      Why?
       Why?
        Why?

I think there is some insight and
    maybe some help for us
        in this astounding word of Jesus
            to these bewildered men.
I repeat:
In full and continual awareness of the reality
    of our human failure and inadequacy,
            in the face
    of our inability to fulfill our hopes and dreams
            and rash promises,
Jesus calls us to new faith in the Father and new faith
            in Himself!
At the point of *old* failure,
Jesus calls us to *new* faith!

            Could it be, then,
that somehow *failure* and *unfaith* go together?
            Could it be, then,
that there is some inner connection between
        faith and *unfailure?*
        Do you suppose that
        when it comes right
            down
              to
              it,
           we fail
        because we lose faith
        in our Father's ability
      to meet all our needs?

Well, we know that was true of our first father
            in the Garden of Eden.
    The tragic fall began with the
            insinuation of doubt:
            "Did God say . . .?"

At the very heart of that first failure
was loss of faith in the Father's provision
for every need—
a reaching out to grasp
what the Father was not trusted to supply.

Which reminds me of a story I can't resist:
God said to Adam, "Why did you do it?"
Adam said, "Eve made me do it."
God said to Eve, "Why did you do it?"
Eve said, "The serpent made me do it."
God said to the serpent, "Why did you do it?"
The serpent said, "I don't have a leg to stand on."
I guess that's our trouble, too.

We know our first father failed because he
let go his faith in the Father.
We also know our Elder Brother, in the wilderness
of His temptation, overcame
precisely because He never let go His faith in His Father!

The tempter insinuated the same doubt
in the wilderness
that he insinuated in the Garden:
"If you are the Son of God . . ."
But our Lord never quit
trusting
or believing in His Father.
That trust was the source of His victory—
a victory, thank God, in which we may share.

I'm thinking that help for our failures comes *not* in
more self-recriminations,
more self-hate,
more promises.

The answer to failure in Christian living is *not*
> more struggles,
> more "try-harders,"
> more "do-betters."

Maybe the answer can be found in
> more faith in the Father,
> more faith in our Lord Jesus,
> more looking away
>> from ourselves
>> and our failures—
>>> to Jesus!

That's where our strength and power really are!
The other day, someone shared this bit of verse from
a minister friend:

> *I* can't.
> He never said I could!
> *He* can.
> And always said He would!
>> *Isn't that beautiful?*

Like Peter, we know what it means
to make rash promises
and declare absolute goals.
And we know what it means
> *to fail!*

What we really need to know, also, is that the
way out
is not more promises
and more unreachable goals—
but more looking away from ourselves,
more trust in God,
more faith in Jesus.
Believe in God, believe also in me.
> That's the word of Jesus Himself.

Well, so endeth the detour.
> *But I'm glad we made it, aren't you?*

Let's move now to Jesus' direct answer
to Peter's question,
"Lord, where are you going?"
The answer given to him and to us all is found in
John 14:2, 3:
**I go to prepare a place for you, and when I
go and prepare a place for you, I will come
again and will take you to myself, that where
I am you may be also.**
That is Jesus' answer.

You know, for too long, when I thought of this
scripture,
I thought simply of Jesus going away
to get a place ready for us,
that He had simply left *this* place and gone to
that place
to get it ready.
And I figured that
if He could make
this wonderful world
in six days—
how beautiful heaven must be!

These days I've been thinking that that really isn't the
point,
at least not the main point.
I am discovering that the "going away" or "departure"
theme
of John's Gospel is a very important one.
It is not only important *that* Jesus went
away—
it is supremely important
how He went away and
why He went away.
*I'm thinking that the manner and the meaning of
His going is the whole point!*

Let's face the question: How did Jesus go away?
You know how He went away?
He went by way of Gethsemane.
He went by way of Calvary.
He went by way of the tomb.
He went by way of the resurrection.
He went by way of the ascension.
He went by way of the exaltation!
That's how He went away!

And then He poured out the Holy Spirit on the Church
testifying that Jesus is Lord! Praise God!
He went away by ultimate encounter with
our ultimate foe!
He went by way of all that the cross means,
by way of all that the resurrection means,
by way of all that the Holy Spirit means.
When death and evil
had done the very worst
that could be done—the mighty
power of God raised Jesus from the
dead and exalted Him at the right hand
of the Father in power and glory! The
poured-out Spirit testifies to His conquering
Lordship forever. And then the promise:

I will come again.

I wish you would hang up in front of you two signs:
On the left-hand sign,
write these words:
I GO AWAY

On the right-hand sign,
write these words:
I WILL COME AGAIN!
Got them?

Can we see that all that we are,
    all that we have,
        the whole of our human existence
                    is between those two signs?
            Between those two great words is the cross!
                Between those two great words, Satan is
ultimately defeated and our redemption
                        is ultimately accomplished.
Sin has been subdued.
    Death has been conquered.
        Hell has been vanquished.
            All the powers of evil have been overcome
                                on that cross.

And can you see the empty tomb
    where the power of God
                        raised Jesus from the dead
                        and exalted Him at the right hand
                                in glory?
                    I go away.
                What a victory He has won!
                    I will come again.
                What a victory He has promised!
I sometimes wonder where we are
                between these two great words of Jesus.
    Are we nearer His coming again
                    than His triumph at the cross?
            Many Christians think so, and maybe we
                                are.

This much is sure:
        We who live "between the times,"
            between these two great words,
                between the signs,
                    live with great assurance and great promise.

We are privileged to live not in our own strength
    but in the strength of Him who has conquered
                                        sin and
                                        death
    and who lives and has poured out His Holy Spirit,
        now present among us in the fellowship
                            of His Church.

And this is why Jesus can say to us
                            weak,
                            human,
                            inadequate types,
        Let not your hearts be troubled!
Jesus said: **Believe in God.**
                    Do you believe in God?
Jesus said: **Believe in me.**
                    Do you believe in Him?
    Then we need to look away from ourselves
                        and look to Him
                        and trust Him.

In and through this whole passage,
    the risen Lord is saying:
                I know who I am.
                I know what I'm doing.
                I know where I'm going.
                I will come again.
                It's all right!
                    I think I need to hear that!
In my humanness and weakness,
    living life "between the times,"
                a new kind of faith is what I need.
                Maybe you do, too.

I don't know where you are on your journey
or what your needs are this day.
  Maybe your dreams have crashed around you.
  Maybe you are experiencing frustration and
    futility,
  Maybe you're walking in the dark
            and don't know what's happening
            or how it's all going to come out.

                            People like you and me
know the meaning of failure and know
    that we do not have the ability in ourselves
      to fulfill our own dreams and hopes. We know
        that we do not have the psychic energy and
        the motivation to be the disciples
                            we want to be.

But, thank God, we can live in hope and share His
    victory!
There is no enemy He has not conquered.
No defeat is ultimate because
            His triumph is ultimate. We can live
            with untroubled hearts in our human
            situation
                        because He is in charge!

                He is Lord! He is Lord!
                He is risen from the dead
                And He is Lord.
                Every knee shall bow;
                Every tongue confess
                That Jesus Christ is Lord.

Father,
our hearts say yes to the Lordship of Jesus.
We bow before you in our humanness
and our weakness.
How often we have failed
and tried harder
and promised more—
and failed again because we were centered
in ourselves.
You have come.
You have triumphed.
And we look away from ourselves–to you!
We thank you that we can live with untroubled hearts—
because you are Lord!
How we need untroubled hearts!
We look to you in trust
and with thanks.
Amen.

Chapter Two

I AM THE ROAD UNDER YOUR FEET

(John 14:4-6)

*One way; Gurus and gods; Stained-glass words;
The Way Himself has come to us.*

Chapter 2

The response of Jesus to Peter's question led
inevitably to the interruption by Thomas.
Jesus had said, in effect,
"I am going to the Father."
Thomas now asked, in effect,
"How do you get there?"
And Jesus answered that question in the classically
beautiful statement:

**I am the way, and the truth, and the life;
no one comes to the Father, but by me.
(John 14:6)**

What beautiful, familiar words!

These words are Jesus' response to one of the
most significant questions we will ever ask,
"How can we know the way?"
And He says,
I am the way, and the truth, and the life.
May I rephrase that?
I am the true way to life!

Jesus is the true way to the Father
because He reveals to us the truth about the Father
and shares with us the life of the Father.
The truth He reveals is the truth that He *is*.
The life that He gives is *Himself*.

The words "No one comes to the Father, but by me"
are not arbitrary negatives.
They do not imply snobbishness or exclusivism.
Jesus does not selfishly lock up all the doors to God
and throw away
the keys!

Only God can open up the way to God.
We don't search for God and find Him for ourselves
over the brow of the hill
or in the meadow
or around the corner.
We do not suddenly come upon God
and say,
"Oh, *there* you are!"

God makes Himself known.
The way *to* God is the way *of* God—
He shows us the *Way*, and the *Way* is Jesus.

I want to pick up a little more on that word *way*.
I wish you would stop now and let your mind run
through the Bible and lift out the verses you can
remember that have the word *way* in them.
I'm sure you can think of several right off!
Some of the old familiar verses in Leviticus
or Numbers or Obadiah! Jeremiah?
Oh, well!

There are several that I've been thinking of:
>Teach me thy *way*, O Lord;
>and lead me on a level path
>because of my enemies.
>>(Psalm 27:11)

>>>Jesus said, **I am the way.**

>Commit your *way* to the Lord;
>trust in him, and he will act.
>>(Psalm 37:5)

>>>Jesus said, **I am the way.**

>Your ears shall hear a word
>behind you, saying,
>"This is the *way*, walk in it."
>>(Isaiah 30:21)

>>>Jesus said, **I am the way.**

>We have turned every one to
>his own *way*.
>>(Isaiah 53:6)

>>>Jesus said, **I am the way.**

I wonder if Jesus was remembering verses like these
when He said, **I am the way.**
I think this verse from Proverbs is also significant:
>There is a *way*
>which seems right to a man,
>but its end is the way to death.
>>(14:12)

I think Jesus was thinking of this
when he answered Thomas.
The way of man is the way of his own choosing—
and it is the way of death!
Jesus alone is the true Way—

and He leads to life!

What do we mean when we say that Jesus is *the Way?*
    We know that He points the way for us—
                        but He is more than a
                            way-pointer.
    He doesn't give us directions and disciplines for
        our journey to God.
    He is not like the gurus of Oriental religions
        who share the secrets of their enlightenment
        and point the way to the god
                    at the top of the mountain.
    He is more than the way to God in the sense that
        Shakespeare is the way to poetry or
        St. Francis is the way to the living of the
                            serving life.
We are closer to the truth when we say that
        Jesus goes with us on the way;
        He is our companion on the journey.

I'm thinking of a verse of an old gospel song:
        He will give me grace and glory;
        And go with me, with me all the way.
It could be, you know, that adherents to
    Oriental religions
        aren't the only ones who put God
        on top of the mountain
            and view Him as a goal to be achieved
                    or an end to be realized.

    I remember a long time ago, when Mary Jo and I
        were pastoring a church in Honolulu,
        a young mother who attended said,
        "Reverend, when I get good enough,
                    I'm going to become a Christian
                    and join your church."

And I'm wondering right now if there is anyone
   reading these words who is saying,
      "When I get strong enough,
         I'm going to enter the victorious life."
      "When I am good enough,
         I'm going to be the Christian I want to be."
      "When I am what I ought to be,
         then I will feel worthy to come to God."
               Jesus has a word for us right here!

The good news of the gospel is that the God of the
mountain
comes
     all
        the
           way
              down
                    to where we are and says:
                      Let me walk with you.

Thank God, there is no reaching up to find Him.
   There is no uphill journey to reach Him.
      He is not up there calling out:
         "Come on up! It's beautiful up here!"
            In infinite, caring love
          He comes all the way to where we are
         and becomes the loving, strengthening
             companion on our journey.

But Jesus, the Way, means even more than this.
   He is more than the *way-pointer;*
      He is more than the companion *on the way;*
        HE *IS* THE WAY!

Somewhere back in the past, while teaching Greek,
I discovered that the word translated *way*
is also the word for *road.*
This fact has given
me a whole new dimension
to what Jesus said about Himself.

To me, the word *way* is a stained-glass word.
It belongs in a church.
Let's put a stained-glass window in the church.
Can you see it?
There is the crown, the flames, the dove.
There are the beautiful muted colors and symbols.
Woven throughout is the banner in Old English letters:

I am the way, and the truth, and the life.

(I can even see the plaque.)
Donated in loving memory of . . .
Somehow the word *road* doesn't fit in that window
very well!
It belongs where our lives are lived.
It belongs to the paths we walk,
the sidewalks of our towns and cities,
the streets and highways of our busy world.
I profoundly believe that Jesus meant His word to be
understood precisely where
our real lives are lived.

I read this somewhere:
Jesus did not say, "At the end of the end of the
way, there you will find me."
He said, **I am the very road under your feet!**
That means that, wherever you are, He is there.
If you are on a mountain, He is there.
If you are in the valley, He is there.

If you are in the pit, He is there.
   He is the road under your feet!

                  Can we ever believe
            that we do not have to come to where He is?
He is where we are.

                  Can we ever trust
            that we do not have to reach up to grasp Him?
He is the road under our feet!

Will anyone ever read these words who feels that
      God is too far away to be found?
            Life too messed up to be straightened out?
         The failure patterns too deeply set to be broken?
The entanglements too complex to be solved?
         The goal so distant that there is no use to try?
                        Don't believe it!
                        That is the devil's lie!

I am not talking about how you feel,
I am not talking about what is complicating your life.
      I just want you to know that
      Jesus is where you are right now—
            feeling what you are feeling,
            thinking what you are thinking,
            experiencing what you are experiencing—
                  where you are,
                  as you are,
                  what you are,
                        right now!

I think St. Augustine understood this,
      and spoke the words we all need to hear:
   "I do not say to thee, Seek a way;
            the Way Himself has come to thee;
                        arise and walk!"

Lord Jesus,
    We try so hard to get where you are—
                    and you have come to us!
            The road under our feet!
    I let my weight down on you.
        I can walk if you are my road and my strength.
        There is hope if you are where I am.
                My Way and my Road, I thank you.
                        Amen.

Chapter Three
SEE FOR YOURSELF
(John 14:7-9)

What is God like? Grandfathers and mechanical monsters; Polaroid panorama; Twenty-five words or less.

Chapter 3

The more I look at these interruptions by the disciples,
the more convinced I am that they are not there
just by accident; nor are they included
just because they happened.
I am convinced that their sequence is of
divine ordering.
The questions asked are, actually, *the* great questions.
Jesus' responses to them are *the* great answers!

First: "Where are you going?"
Then: "How can we know the way?"
Now Philip's probing request,
Lord, show us the Father, and
we shall be satisfied. (John 14:8)

Philip was a good Jew.
He had heard about God all his life.
From a child he had known the Scriptures.
He had a God-language;
understood God-talk;
used God-words.

Yet some hunger in him, dormant
through those years of rote religion,
was called to life by the presence and ministry of Jesus.
Out of the depths of his soul came the haunting
question,
"What is God like?"

Though Philip had heard about God all his life,
he was still unsatisfied,
because he did not know God as Father!
You know, it is one thing
to know *about* God,
to know God-words.
It is quite another to know God as Father.
And it is only in Jesus, the Son, that we can know
God, the Father.
"Show us the Father, and we shall be satisfied."
How true!
I'm thinking that if we
knew God as Father as Jesus knew Him,
we would indeed be satisfied!

For Jesus, the Fatherhood of God was
no commonplace, dull and dusty theological fact.
For Jesus, the Fatherhood of God was
His life
and breath
and soul!
He lived in obedience to His Father.
He lived in full dependence upon His Father.
He spoke with the authority of His Father.
He died in the will of His Father.
He was raised by the power of His Father!

I'm wondering if I'm writing to anyone who,
          like Philip,
    has known about God for years
     but has not really known Him as Father.
        I wonder if behind the God-words,
        underneath the God-talk,
    there is a hungering *unknowing* of the Father.
That unknowing takes the shape of dissatisfaction
    and unfulfillment that haunts your days
     and surrounds your times of devotion.
         How sad to know God-language
         without knowing God as Father!

When you come
     right down to it,
       the joy,
       the satisfaction,
       the authority,
       the confidence—
   all these things that we need and want—
are intimately related to our real fellowship with God
         as our Father.
   Hiding underneath Philip's request
    was the question
     "What is God like?"
       I am coming to believe more
       certainly than ever in my life
   that this is the fundamental question for all of us.

The fundamental question for folks like us is not,
      "Does God exist?"
        We believe that He exists.
        We may have our moments
       of doubting and unfeeling and
       wondering. We have our questions
      as we face the mystery of our humanness
      and the reality of evil and the sometimes
     absurd, irrational events of our lives.

But these times are not permanent.
We come back to our moorings.
Our faith is pretty well anchored
                    in the reality of God.
            But we do have a problem about God.
                And I think it is a very serious one.

Our question is, *"What is God like?"*
                I think there is no way to tell you
            how important I think that question is!

And I am not so naive as to assume that
        all of us have the same quality of understanding.
            Many of us, brought up in the care and teaching
                            of the church,
                    have some ideas about God that
                        are positively weird!

If I could, I would give you a 3 by 5 card
    with this question at the top: WHAT IS GOD LIKE?
I would ask you to take a minute or two,
        and in 25 well-chosen words,
            answer the question.
                    Since we are talking about it,
                    why don't you go ahead and do it?

And, while you are writing, let me talk with you.
        I think that the way you answer the question on
        that card
        is fundamental to the way you answer
                all the other big questions of your life!

I want to illustrate that with a couple of episodes
        that happened some years ago. I mention them
            because they have become symbols,
        and in other forms,
                have been repeated over and over and over!

I remember a troubled girl who came to see me
    one day in my office at school. She dropped
        into a chair and, ready to cry, exclaimed,
            "I don't like me!"
                        (Looking at her, I
                        felt like saying,
                    "I don't blame you!")
                 But of course I didn't!!

Then we began to talk and, pretty soon,
   the conversation drifted around
      to the subject of God.
"Sometimes I think God is like my grandmother," she
   said, "and that's good,
                 because my grandmother is neat!
But most of the time, I think God is like my
                  grandfather."
"That's *not* so neat?"
"No! He comes
   from a long line of Prussian army officers!"
                     When she said that,
             a light went on in my little head.
                 Let me rephrase that.
             A little light went on in my head.
       Depression,
       frustration,
       low self-estimate,
       guilt,
       unhappiness—
                 she knew them all.
And underneath them all—
   not actually causing them all—
      was a *very bad* image of God!
Her God was sometimes like gentle, loving
                    grandmother;
mostly like strict, stern, disciplinarian grandfather.

Do you see now how
faith
and trust
and obedience
    are affected by our understanding of God?
I remember that Martin Luther had a hard time
       with the Lord's Prayer.
 When he said the words "Our Father," he thought
      of his own father
    and then I guess he thought of the devil,
     and he didn't want to pray anymore!
     I wonder how many others are like that!

Then I remember a long time ago when I was preaching
 in a church in Globe, Arizona,
     (I'm sure you've been there many times)
I talked with a woman whose husband had left her
 and a son of about four or five years of age.
 After church one evening, she began to talk about
      her doubts and fears,
      her trouble and pain,
      her loneliness and heartache,
      questions about God's goodness,
       and *does He really care?*
After awhile, I asked her,
  "Have you ever gone out under the stars,
   or knelt down by your bed,
   and told God all the things you are telling me?"
I will never forget her answer!
  "Oh, no! There are just some things
       you don't tell God!"
        Really?

A few months later I saw her at a camp meeting.
 On the pathway
  between the tabernacle and the cabins,
      we talked.

The preacher had been laying on us some of the great
words:

Yield to God.
Obey God.
Surrender to God.
Give everything to God.
And she was having problems.

She said:

"I can give myself to God.
But I can't give my little boy to God.
God can do whatever He wants with me.
But I can't give my boy to Him."

I'm not sure, but I probably picked up where
the preacher left off:

Love God.
Trust God.
Surrender to God.
Yield everything to God.
Give your boy to God.
"But I can't!"
"Why not?"
"Because I'm afraid God will take him!"
That was when another light went on in my head!
I was pouring out to her the good words,
the big words,
the beautiful words,
the life-changing
words.
And they were all sounding like
the bad words,
the hard words,
the dark words,
the impossible words,
because her mental image of God was bad!

I read somewhere that a false *mental* image of God
is just as bad as a false *metal* image of God.
                                        I believe that!

Shall we go back and listen to those two persons
    talking on the pathway:
                "Give everything to God.
                Give your boy to God."
                        "I can't."
                        "You must."
                        "I cannot."
                        "Why not?"
"I'm afraid God will take him!"

Can we see that the whole situation on both sides is
    conditioned by the mental image of God?
    One saw God as the loving Father to whom
            all things great and small could be entrusted.
    The other saw Him as an unfeeling, mechanical
            monster
    whose cold, steel hand was programmed to scoop
        up the precious gift she was commanded to offer.
                I think if I felt that way about God,
                I wouldn't want to trust Him either!

Maybe I don't need to say this,
        but I'm thinking that if we move the conversation
        off the camp meeting path and into the church,
            surround it with sentimental music—
                sweet organ sounds and songs of
                dedication—
    that mother might shed some tears and be persuaded—
    to make some act of reponse or say the expected words,
                    but nothing would really be changed.
            Inside, her image of God would remain the same.

I must admit that we preachers don't help people much
with their image of God in times of sorrow or loss
or death.
Ever hear words like these
at the funeral of a child?

"God saw this little rosebud one day—
so perfect, so fragrant—and He wanted
it for His heavenly garden. So He reached
down and plucked it and planted it to bloom
in heaven."

How awful!
How pagan!

God is no Sovereign Gardener who sees,
desires,
and snatches
in death!
We can safely
love God,
trust God,
believe in God,
give everything to God.

Well, all of this is to remind us
that the 25 well-chosen words
we have written on the 3 by 5 cards
are supremely important
to the whole of our lives.
It really matters what we think of God.

What is God like?
Jesus said,
He who has seen me has seen the Father.
God is like Jesus!

Now, would you turn your card over
and look at the question on the other side?

The first question was, "What is God like?"
The second is, "Where did you get that idea?"
It is not only important *what* we
think of God; it is also important
where we get our thoughts of Him!

It is almost frightening to realize that we gather up
data that determines
our most fundamental decisions
in an offhand,
casual,
almost accidental manner.

How often we have heard
people in prayer groups
and Bible groups
and Sunday School classes
begin to make some profound conclusions
with such words as:
"I've always thought that . . ."
"We were taught in our home that . . ."
"I heard a preacher say once . . ."

And here is the classic one:
"Isn't there a verse in the Bible somewhere
that says something about . . ."
It turns out that some of the most
significant concepts by which we live
have been collected
at
random.

Can it be that our ideas of God grow that way?
I've wondered if maybe we all have a sort of spiritual
Polaroid camera
with which we take snapshots
of certain events or situations in our lives
and thereby gather up our ideas of God.

When we lived in Pasadena,
we had a family room with a bulletin board
on one wall.
We tacked and pinned all kinds of things on that board:
the cat and dog sleeping together like
friends,
Rob's basketball team,
Susan's choir pictures,
snaps from our last vacation,
an invitation to a wedding—
all these formed a friendly collage of family "stuff."
When we moved into our house in San Diego,
we gave the whole thing a little more class.
We selected some better family pictures,
had them framed,
and hung them on the wall in style.
The friendly "junk stuff" ended up
stuck to the refrigerator with magnets!
I've been thinking
that somewhere in the back room
of the soul,
there must be a bulletin board labeled "GOD."
Through the years, we have collected
various impressions,
sermon phrases,
Bible stories,
life events,
crisis times,
and tacked them to the board in
what has become
a collage of our God-image.

A tragedy happens in a godly family.
Click!
Why did God let that happen?
A bad picture goes on the board.

You read the Old Testament story of Moses
 and Pharaoh,
get the idea that God hardened Pharaoh's
 heart, then
turned around and clobbered him for it.
          Click!
       What's going on here?
      Another negative picture.

A father beats his children.
Click!
Someone in church gets sick and everyone prays,
but the prayed-for person dies.
Click!

    Someone in church gets sick.
    Everyone prays and the person
     recovers.
          Click!
        That's better!

Someone has a remarkable conversion experience.
Click! Click!
That's much better!

     A church member starts tithing
         and gets rich!
        All right, Lord!
   And we use a whole roll of film!

 Love God. Trust God. Obey God.
 Give everything to God.
    The collage is balancing out, and
    the big words are sounding better.

Can we see what is happening?
 We are gathering up data from
   the experiences of our lives
   and constructing our own ideas of God
        out of them.
        How tragic!

If our lives are good—our God is good.
If our lives are bad—our God is bad.

All of us know someone who has said something
     like this:
          "Don't talk to me about God!
               My mother got sick and I prayed
          for her to be healed.
               But God didn't care—and she died.
                    Don't talk to me about God!"

On the other hand, there are those whose view of God
     is shallow and sentimental:
               "He is so wonderful because He answers
               all my prayers and solves all my problems
               and gives me so much happiness."
                              I wonder what
                         they say when trouble comes?!

It makes all the difference *what we think of God.*
It makes all the difference *where we get our ideas of God.*
It is one thing to gather up data and develop
                              our own image of God.
     It is quite another to allow God *to reveal Himself* in
               a self-portrait—His Son, our Lord Jesus.
Well, what sorts of pictures do you have on your board?
     Will you let the Holy Spirit clear them away and
          replace them with a picture of the
                              New Testament Jesus?
     Or are you holding on to God-pictures that are
                    inaccurate and destructive—
                    childhood images,
                    adolescent memories,
                    outdated mementos?

These images are so often false
and
distorted
that it is impossible to see God
as He wants to be seen—
in the person of Jesus Christ.
Everything, in the final analysis,
hangs on this one peg:
God is like Jesus!

I guess we really don't need 25 words to answer
the questions on our 3 by 5 card.
We only need one.

What is God like?
Jesus.
Where did we get that idea?
From Jesus.

I'm hearing again the big words:
Love God.
Obey God.
Trust God.
Give everything to God.
If God is like Jesus, then
they are the good words,
the beautiful words,
the life-transforming words—
and to them—
and to the Christlike God,
my heart is saying—Yes! Yes! Yes!

Yes, Jesus, yes.
If God is like you, my heart says yes!
But it is hard to let go old ideas
and feelings
and images.

Give us grace to bring them all to you.
Let your Holy Spirit cleanse,
change,
edit,
replace
the false and destructive God-thoughts
we have carried so long—
and fill our hearts and minds with the
vision of yourself.
Amen.

Chapter Four
I AM REAL
(John 14:22-23)

Sky blue and red hot; Do-able deeds; The incredible key.

Chapter 4

The wonder of Judas' question is that it brings
all the realities exposed by the previous questions
into the realm of personal experience.
Judas asks Jesus: "How will you manifest yourself
to us and not to the world?"
or, to phrase the question in third person,
"How does Jesus become real to us?"
Peter wanted to know where his Lord was going.
Thomas wanted to know how to get there.
Philip wanted to know what God is like.

These three question-answers
express the great central truths
of the gospel:
Jesus is Lord.
He is the way to the Father.
He is the revelation of the Father.

But Judas' question remains:
"How does Jesus become real *to us?*"
(Maybe this question belongs
at the end of this chapter,
but I can't help asking it now,
"Is Jesus real to you?")

We know it is possible to believe
the great truths without internalizing them
to hold to great realities that are not real to us,
to know *about* Jesus without knowing *Him*.
How do we know God?
How does He become real?

Maybe, somewhere, it needs to be said
that this question meets us
wherever we are on our journey.
Some of us have heard the doctrines,
but they have never "come alive" in us.
Some of us have really come to know Christ,
but His Lordship has been prohibited from
certain hidden areas of our lives. We have
posted "Keep Out" signs and have forbidden Him
to enter and to take over.
Some of us have had all kinds of religious experiences,
but the truths have not been behaviorized very well.
In other words, *no one could tell by looking!*
Someone once asked this penetrating question:
"If you were tried in a court of law
for living the Christian life,
would there be enough evidence to convict you?"

More important than Judas' question, though,
is the answer of Jesus:

If a man loves me, he will keep my word,
and my Father will love him, and
we will come to him
and make our home with him.
(John 14:23)

Did Jesus say, "If a man loves me,
        he will have an 'emotional experience'?"
           or
      "If a man loves me, he will be able to
         perform some great spiritual work?"

I'm sensitive at this point and
    hesitant to write about it because I believe so much
      in the reality and validity of personal experience.
        But I'm going ahead to write, because I believe
      that experiences can be removed from truth
        and because I believe that the sensuous
          atmosphere of our society
          has weighted the scales
            in favor of emotionalism.

We do live in a sensual age, you know.
    We are conditioned by the advertising media
      to want good vibes,
            pleasant feelings,
              exciting sensations.
                Salesmen use touch,
                    taste,
                    sound,
                    smell,
                    sight,
                    erotic stimuli
as tools in their selling game.
    Everything from tractors to toothpaste,
        soup to sewing machines,
            is offered sensuously.

It's foolish to think that we are not affected by all this.
    Ours is not only a sensuous age physically and
    materially,

it is a sensuous age spiritually.
I believe there is such a thing as "spiritual sensualism."

We want the Holy Spirit to lift us up like the tide
and set us down in some fantastic experience!
We want to be sky blue and red hot!
We want to be ready to go!
No doubts.
No questions.
Just praise the Lord!
"How are you?"
"Fantastic!"
(You can't even say "Fine!" anymore.)
We want a gospel experience that brings us
emotion and joy and *fantastic!*
We want that.

Now, I don't mind saying "we,"
because while my head knows that's kind of dumb,
my heart really *likes* fantastic.
I enjoy chills
up
and
down
my spine
as much as you do!
I like to feel blessed, and
I like to get all charged up, and
I like to float around on cloud nine!
I felt that way once.
I never will forget it!

But what I'm hearing in Jesus' word to Judas is that
we don't need another newer, deeper, greater
experience.

What we really need is
> genuine,
> careful,
> deliberate
> obedience to that which we have
> > already experienced!

So when I talk about obedience,
> I'm not really talking about what we can't
> > understand
> > or what we can't do.
> I'm not talking about those words of Jesus
> > that are too much for us.
> What bothers me are the words that are
> > understandable and do-able!
> > > *Are you catching on?*
What is disturbing me in my own life is
> that it is so difficult to let the words of Jesus
> > > come
> > > down

> into my daily conversation,
> > my daily patterns of thoughts
> > > and responses
> > > > and reactions
> > > > and decisions.

Mary Jo and I have been married a long time now,
> and everyone knows that
> > in a good long-term relationship,
> > > there have to be some ground rules.
> > > > Well, you will be glad to know
> > > that we have established the ground rules
> > and firmed up the guidelines at our house.
> > > *I make the big decisions and*
> > > *she makes the little ones! Amen!*

I make the *big* decisions:

> How are we going to handle the energy
> crisis?
> How are we going to reestablish the moral
> strength of our government?
> What are we going to do about the ecology
> crisis!

She makes the *little* decisions:

> Where are we going to live?
> How are we going to spend our money?
> What am I going to do with my time?
>> *We let God make the big decisions,*
>> *and we make the little ones!*

The words of Jesus need to be let in
> to the attitudes
>> and responses
>> and reactions
>>> and decisions
>>>> of daily life.
>>>>> It is in this process that
>>>>> our gracious Father
>>>> makes Himself known to us
>>>>> in loving intimacy.
>>>>>> *How incredible!*

We can know God, the Father,
>> both in fact and in person!
>>> And the key to this knowledge
>>>> is *obedience!*
>>> This greatest of all knowing
>>> is not ours by virtue of some
>>> marvelous spiritual achievement
>>> nor fantastic spiritual experience,
>>> but *by simple, loving obedience.*

There is a beautiful promise contained
    in Jesus' answer to Judas. In this promise
        Jesus places our knowledge of God in the context
            of love and home.
      **My Father will love him, and we will come
      to him and** *make our home with him.* **(14:23)**

Throughout the Bible there is
    a wonderful harmony of God and home.
      When God created man
        He did not set him in isolation,
            but in community,
                in a family.
        God promised Abraham a family—
   and Abraham became the father of a great nation.
      God revealed Himself to Hosea
        as the forgiving husband and father
            of His wayward people.
      God sent His Son, Jesus Christ,
        to gather us into the family of God,
          to make us all brothers and sisters in Him,
           to provide us a beautiful earthly home,
         and to make ready for us a home in heaven.

Our knowledge of God is not unrelated to all of this.
    The beautiful verse in Revelation communicates the
same message:
            Behold, I stand at the door and knock;
            **if any one hears my voice and opens the
            door,**
            I will come in to him and eat with him,
                and he with me. (3:20)

I read somewhere that people of all places and all times
    have always found that coming to Jesus
              is like coming *home!*
              Is Jesus real to you?

Thank God, there is a handle;
   there is a place to begin;
      there is a point of contact.
                        Begin to obey
                     simply and honestly
                     those words of Jesus
                     that you understand—
                     those that speak clearly
            to your situation and your needs.
Because I believe,
with all my heart,
that the promise is true:
         He will come home with us!

Oh Jesus,
         You have made God clear to us.
               You have brought Him near to us
                     and made Him dear to us
                        and we thank you!
      We want to know you,
            to be at home with you,
               to fellowship with you.
Teach us that it all begins by our
         simple obedience to your words.
Lord, we really do need to listen!
                  Help us, we pray. Amen.

Chapter Five

DON'T QUIT NOW

(John 15:1-27)

Growing over the wall; Oranges, lemons, and
"pruning"; Out of the cage; "Hang in there,
Baby!" We really do need a garage sale!

Chapter 5

The fifteenth chapter of John has been called
the "Discourse on Relationships."
In the first paragraph, Jesus talks to His disciples
about their relationship with Him (vv. 1-11);
in the second, He talks about their relationship
with each other (vv. 12-17);
and in the third, He talks of their relationship
with the hostile world (vv. 18-27).

I am especially concerned with the first paragraph.
What does Jesus say about our relationship with
Him?
What does it mean in our lives?
Here are some of His words:
I am the true vine, and my Father
is the vinedresser.
Every branch of mine that bears no fruit,
he takes away, and every branch that does
bear fruit he prunes, that it may bear more fruit.

I am the vine, you are the branches.
He who abides in me, and I in him,
he it is that bears much fruit,
for apart from me you can do nothing.
(vv. 1-5)

The vine has been the symbol
  of Israel's religious heritage for a long, long time.
    Israel pictured herself as the vineyard of the Lord
          or a noble vine of God's own planting.
    Prophets referred to Israel as the tender vine
that God had removed from Egypt and
  transplanted in the
      land of Canaan with the intention that
          it take root,

              grow,

                  and flourish,
          covering the world with

                  grace,

                      blessing,

                          and healing.
Here is the sad thing:
    Israel, the vine of God's planting,
        never did become the missionary people
            through whom God could bless the world.
                              It never
                          grew over the wall!

So Isaiah declared that Israel was a vineyard run wild!
    Jeremiah complained that Israel was a degenerate
                    plant of a strange vine,
        and Hosea mourned that Israel was an empty
                                vine!
Maybe it is out of this background that Jesus
  proclaimed:
              I am the true vine.

His roots are in the very
heart of God
and his love, grace, and healing
reach out to cover the world.
As the true Vine,
He is the bearer of the life of God to
every one of us.

But I think the incredible thing is the next line:
You are the branches.
He is the Vine;
we are the branches!

How beautiful!
Jesus uses the relationship He has with the Father
as the analogy of our relationship
with each other and with Himself.

What an awesome thing!
It is expressed specifically in verses 9 and 10:
As the Father has loved me,
so have I loved you; abide in my love.
If you keep my commandments,
you will abide in my love,
just as I have kept my Father's commandments
and abide in His love.

As the Father's love is toward the Son,
So the Son's love is toward us.
As the Son abides through obedience,
So we abide in the Son's love through obedience.

I think we would never have had the audacity
to use this intimate relationship as an analogy
for our own relationship with our Lord Jesus Christ.
But I'm glad *He* did!

The beautiful imagery in these verses is
                                    "vine and branches."
    I think the fundamental result of the vine-branch
                            relationship is "fruitfulness . . ."
        Verse 2 speaks of "bears no fruit,"
                                "does bear fruit,"
                                        "bear more fruit."

        Verses 5 and 8 exhort us to
                            "bear much fruit."

Maybe it's because I grew up on the farm,
    but the idea of bearing fruit is very appealing to me.
                                Whatever it means,
                            I want to be a fruitful person.
I'm realizing that I don't know much about
                        "bearing fruit."
                                How do we define it?

Galatians 5:22 defines the "fruits of the Spirit"
                    in terms of love,
                                joy,
                                peace,
                                patience,
                                kindness,
                                goodness,
                                faithfulness,
                                gentleness,
                                self-control.
Paul speaks of bearing fruit
                    in every good work and increasing
                    in the knowledge of God.
                            (Colossians 1:10)
                    and of
                                being filled with the fruits of
                                righteousness.
                                    (Philippians 1:11)

Maybe fruit-bearing means reproduction in kind—
   as in orange trees reproducing oranges
     or people reproducing other people
        or Christians reproducing Christians.
However defined, whether it refers to
          growth in grace
          or productivity
          or maturity
          or life
          or joy
          or juice
          or abundance
          or increase . . .
                whatever it is, I want it!
                    And you do, too!
We know this much: Jesus was a fruitful person.
   And His great concern was for the fruitfulness
      of the infant body of believers to whom
      He poured out His heart that night.
In this paragraph Jesus speaks of several things
         that seem to be intimately related to
            fruit-bearing.
For one thing, Jesus says that fruit-bearing
     involves submission to the pruning process.

I grew up in central California on a citrus ranch.
   My dad raised oranges and lemons.
        I never learned much about "pruning"!
When we lived in Pasadena and had a few grapevines,
     the pruning projects were usually disastrous—
       no fruit the next year,
         then very small fruit the following year.
But I recall that our pruning of the citrus trees
  was for two reasons:
      one was to cut away the dead branches
      that had been frostbitten during the winter;

another was to cut out the suckers which
looked lush and green, but drained the
precious life juices from the trees
and kept them from producing any fruit.

I guess grapes are pruned for the same reasons.
Fruit is produced on new growth;
the old branches hinder the flow of life to the
new stock.
As my old Granddad would say:
Are you catching on?

God wants to teach us
that the things we let go are no less significant
for our fruitfulness than the things we
grasp and keep!

Did you ever have a garage sale?
Or need to have one?
Come to think of it,
those are two very foolish questions!

At school one day, one of the professors
told of a famous ichthyologist
who knew the names of thousands of fish.
But he came to a time in his life
when he discovered that
if he learned the name of a new student,
he forgot the name of an old fish!
I think I understand that.

Most of the time, my garage is in that condition—
if anything *new* goes in,
something *old* has got to go out!
Sometimes the parting is painful!

We finally sold our tandem bike . . .
    I bought it for Mary Jo and myself to
        have fun on and stay healthy with.
            I rode on the front;
            she rode on the back.
      She never did comment much on the view!
And we rode that bike just enough to get sore!
    Legs hurt too much to stand!
    Bottoms hurt too much to sit!
I hung it in the garage with nylon rope and pulleys
           and it collected dust
           and seldom came down.
   It was painful—but it really needed to go.
           Like other things, it not only
        cluttered the garage,
      it cluttered our minds
     and used up psychic energy.
Every time we saw that bike,
   though no words were spoken,
     both thoughts and emotions were stirred.
          Are we going to ride it?
              When?
              Where?
              Why?
            Why not?
Defensive thoughts!
   Conflicting emotions!
     It was painful—but it really needed to go!

What a small *thing*.
Yet the bike became the symbol for all the other *things:*
        boats,
          trailers,
            tools,
              clothes,
                cars, etc. etc. etc.

We keep spending,
   gathering up,
     holding on . . .
        We gather things and
         collect activities until
   we are too busy to use our gathered things—
or get another job to pay for them!

We pick up attitudes,
   and habits
    and relationships
       that draw off our energies
      and sap our strength
    and then wonder why we aren't joyful,
       and growing,
       and productive.
I'm thinking, too, about
    things we read,
    things we watch,
    things we think about.
I am wondering about some folks—
   do they ever, ever have other thoughts
     than thoughts of sports or,
      making money,
      or buying things?

I am thinking about our spiritual concepts—
    our ideas of God,
     the Bible,
      church.
  How many of us have minds and hearts filled
with childhood's leftover notions—
  cluttered with outmoded concepts,
    outgrown hurts,
     obsolete perceptions?

    And the clutter grows . . .

There is no room for fresh, new,
understanding attitudes—new fruit!
You know, we really do need a garage sale!

The Greek word for *prune* in verse 2 is the same word
for *clean* in verse 3. In English the word is *catharsis*.
(You don't suppose that's why they call *prunes prunes*,
do you?)
Surely not!

We learn in John 15 that our pruning, cleansing process
comes through obedience to the words of Jesus
in the same way Jesus' pruning process came about—
through obedience to His Father's word.
Think of all Jesus could have done—
and didn't!
Think of all Jesus could have had—
and didn't!
But how much He did accomplish because
He didn't try to do everything!
How much He really had because
He didn't have so much!

Sometimes we need to back away and take a good look
at our life-style and ask,
"Jesus, do you have anything to say about all this?"

Have you ever experienced times when
there emerges a hunger for a change in yourself
and your style of life—
your house,
your schedule,
your relationships,
the frantic, mad pace?
Have you ever had the feeling—
there must be a better way?

I believe these times of discontent
are God-given times to be quiet and
obediently listen to the words of Jesus.
They are times to yield to His pruning.

Does His Word expose a restricting habit?
　　Does His Word point out a destructive relationship
　　　　　　　　　　　　that needs to be broken?
　　　　Is life filled with so much that it is cluttered—
　　　　　　　　　　　　　　and barren?
　　　　　　　　　　Jesus, what is your word to me?

　　　　Who knows when a hobby becomes a master, or
　　　　　a possession becomes a passion,
　　　　　　　or recreation becomes non-recreative?
(I probably mention things like boats and trailers
　　　　　　　　　　　because I want a little sailboat
　　　　　　　　　　　　　and can't afford it
　　　　　　　　　　and I am not willing to sell my trailer
　　　　　　　　　　　　　to buy one!)
So we really do need to listen to the words of Jesus.
　　　Obedience to these words is the pruning process
　　　　　　　　　　that brings true fruitfulness.
I'm realizing anew, even as I am writing these words,
that though we are able to rationalize almost anything
we can afford or really want,
　　　　　　　the words of Jesus lead us to the joy-pain
　　　　　　　　　　of surrender to the pruning—
　　　　　　　　and *obedience brings abundance!*

Hear another big word from this passage from Jesus—
　　　　　　not only pruning but praying.
　　If you abide in me, and my words abide in you,
　　　ask whatever you will, **and it shall be done**
　　　　for you. By this my Father is glorified,
　　　　　so that you bear much fruit, and so
　　　　　　prove to be my disciples. (15:7-8)

I wish I knew how to understand fully these words:
Ask whatever you will, and it will be done for you.
I know that the Man who gave us these
words did not get
the answer He wanted to the most
agonizing prayer He ever prayed;
My Father, if it be possible,
let this cup pass from me.
(Matthew 26:39)

Yet Jesus lived in a confident, prayerful relationship
with His Father and passes on to us
that same kind of attitude. He tells us
to ask confidently, trustfully
for whatever we want.
That's not the final word about prayer,
but it certainly is the *first* word about it!
We are told to ask for whatever we want!
Sometimes we ask hesitantly,
"Is it all right to ask God for . . .?"
"Is it all right to pray about . . .?"
Do you suppose we can ever learn that there is nothing,
nothing,
nothing,
about which we cannot pray?!
Whatever we are thinking, we best be praying!
If you are thinking it—be praying it:
Things refined or gross,
clean or sordid,
light or dark . . .
what we think,
what we desire,
what we feel—
all should be opened up to God.
That is the only way our relationship to the Father
can be like our Lord's relationship—
utterly honest and open.

Have you ever heard couples say,
     "We share everything!
        There are no secrets between us!
           Our relationship is absolutely
                    open!''
             Well, don't believe it totally!
There is no way we can be utterly open with each other!
             We have too much to lose!

But everything—everything
        can be opened up to God!
I've been thinking about it this way:
  If there are desires in us that are worthy,
               unworthy,
               trivial,
               profound,
               beautiful,
               ugly,
               spiritual,
               materialistic,
       and we place a filter over them
      and only allow certain desires
    to come through in the form of prayer,
     then we are living
      at two levels.

We all have thoughts and desires deep within us,
   and we don't know if we should or should not pray
                  about them.
   They have to do with
       our homes,
       our work,
       our school life,
       how we are being treated,
       how we are being loved or not loved,
       affirmed or not affirmed.

Here are all these desires.
     What if we put a grid over them and only let
        the "worthy"ones out of the "cage"
          in the form of prayer?
What would happen to the cageful of real
                  thoughts and
                  feelings and
                  desires—
                      unshared,
                      unopened,
                      unprayed?
What God wants us to do is take away the grid,
          to uncover the cage,
             to let it all out
                in prayer.

     Are they worthy desires?
       Lord, you call it!
     Are they selfish ambitions?
       Lord, what do you say?
I believe profoundly that only as all our desires
are opened up to God.
     can they be known,
         cleansed,
         edited—
              so that change and
              growth and
              insight and
              fruitfulness can
              come in!

If we pray only our holy prayers—
     our unholy thoughts remain unholy still—
     and pace the cage, feeding on our
             fantasies and daydreams.
       And sometimes—
         they grow strong enough
        to break out and wreak havoc!

Then a "holy" person can do an "unholy" thing.
And we wonder:
How can that be?
It is because the "unacceptable" thoughts and
hungers and
desires and
yearnings
were not truly opened up to God for His
renewing,
cleansing,
healing grace!
Whatever you desire, don't define it beforehand.
Pour it all out to God, and His Spirit
will define and edit and cleanse.
I am hearing the word of Jesus:
If you abide in me
and my words abide in you,
ask whatever you will . . .
We are to pray.
He will filter.
It is part of God's way to fruitfulness.
I want to write one more word related to our
fruit-bearing—
it is the word *abide*.
Three times it is used in this short paragraph:
Abide in me and I in you. (v. 4)
Abide in me and my words abide in you. (v. 7)
Abide in my love. (v. 9)

In an earlier chapter, I said that the word *way* was
a stained-glass word.
Abide is that kind of word.
It has an "in church" sound
and belongs on the banner
printed in Old English
in the Gothic window.

Looks beautiful
with the light shining through.
But it really doesn't belong there
because it actually means *stay* as in "Sit!"
"Stay!"
It means *remain*.

If, instead of a cathedral, we were to build
a Jesus-People-Tabernacle-House-Church,
we would put in a window with that familiar poster
that shows the cat hanging on the line with
the caption: "Hang in there, Baby!"

That's what *abide* really means.
And it seems to me that our Lord ties abiding
and fruit-bearing
together in a way that gives hope to us all.

I've been thinking about what it is that
makes the difference between
those who begin the Christian journey and quit—
and those who begin and don't quit . . .
Ever wondered about that?

My guess is that, if all those who had come in
the front door of your church in the last ten years
had stayed—
and none had left
through the back door,
your church would be far larger than it is today.
(And I don't mean those who left town!)
Some folks come into the faith and stay and grow.
Some begin with a lot of pizazz and just drop out.
I've wondered why.
Are some folks religious by nature
and some irreligious?

I used to think you could spot religious people—
then I went to a general assembly in our church
        and found I could only tell them
                by their delegate badges!
                (Well, that's almost true!)
I used to think there were preacher types—
then I went to a preachers' meeting
        and saw every personality type
                under the sun!
Some folks think there is a preacher's *wife* type!
    I remember a ministerial student at school
    who was in love with this lovely girl—
    but worried that she didn't fit the image
                of a minister's wife.
        I wanted to hit him over the head with some
    large, blunt object to get his attention,
        and then yell: "No! No! No!"
                Well, I've concluded that people don't go
                        or stay
                because of personality type.

Then maybe those who begin the journey and
    hang in there
            are those who, by some providence of God,
                have been spared the real and heavy
                        sorrows of life.
    They stay because the "grass is greener over here"—
        they haven't had to struggle
        with pain and doubt and tragedy.
                                No way!
God's people know all about those things, don't they?

So what keeps them staying, abiding?
I think I have found the answer, finally.
        The folks who begin and keep on going
                are the ones who don't quit!

The answer to a fruitful life is abiding,
staying,
remaining,
hanging in there!

Abide in me.
Abide in my love.
Abide in me and my words abide in you.

The wonder and beauty of it all
is that fruitfulness is not for the special,
virile few.
It comes to us in the same way it came to Jesus:
He submitted to His Father's pruning,
opened His whole heart to His Father in prayer,
and didn't quit!
I am feeling, as I write these words,
that there is hope for me, too!

Lord,

there is hope for us and we thank you.
We want so much to be fruitful.
We need so much help in our praying
and in our obeying.
Remind us again that we really belong to you
and we share your very life.
Help us to stay in your love
and to stay in your words.
Help us just to stay—
and not quit!
In Jesus' name.
Amen.

Chapter Six

HELP IS ON HIS WAY

(John 14:15-17, 26; 15:26; 16:7-15)

No security blanket; Side by side; Tri-theism and trinitarianism; Getting our Gods together.

Chapter 6

In an earlier chapter I shared my conviction
that we do not all have a common, clear
understanding of the character of God.
Some of us carry around ideas
of God that are totally at odds
with His self-revelation in Jesus.
Many of us have false mental images
that are destructive to our wholeness and joy.

We really do need to listen
to Jesus' words about His Father
and to see in Him the revelation of the Father.
But I've been thinking—
these same words could be written
about our understanding of the Holy Spirit
with the addition of a *"How much more . . . !"*

When I tell a church congregation that I am going
to speak from the words of Jesus
about the Holy Spirit,
the response usually comes
in three sets of vibrations:

Some of them say, "Oh, yes! Let's do it!"
Some of them say, "Oh, no! Not that!"
Most of them say, "Oh, well . . ."

Could it be that our neutral or negative feelings
about the Holy Spirit persist because we have not
listened carefully to what Jesus had to say?
Is it possible
that, here and there,
we have picked up thoughts and images
and concepts and emotions about the Spirit
without ever having brought them to Jesus?

Shall we do that together right now?
Though we usually turn to Acts and the writings of Paul
for information about the Holy Spirit,
Jesus spoke some words about the Spirit
and His ministry
that we mustn't miss!
And I believe Jesus is a reasonable authority!

In the Farewell Discourses, there are
four distinct statements about the Holy Spirit
which directly relate to the Christian life.
Let's look at them:
**If you love me, you will keep my commandments.
And I will pray the Father, and he will give you
another Counselor, to be with you for ever, even
the Spirit of truth, whom the world cannot receive,
because it neither sees him nor knows him; you
know him, for he dwells with you.**
(John 14:15-17)
**But the Counselor, the Holy Spirit, whom the
Father will send in my name, he will teach you all
things, and bring to your remembrance all that
I have said to you. (v. 26)**

**But when the Counselor comes, whom I shall send
to you from the Father, even the Spirit of truth,
who proceeds from the Father, he will bear witness
to me. (15:26)**

**Nevertheless I tell you the truth: it is to your
advantage that I go away, for if I do not go away,
the Counselor will not come to you; but if I go, I
will send him to you . . . When the Spirit of truth
comes, he will guide you into all the truth . . .
He will glorify me, for he will take what is mine
and declare it to you. (16:7-15)**

Let's begin by looking at the terms Jesus uses when
    speaking of the Spirit.
        What does Jesus call Him?
        What is His name?
    In each of the sayings, Jesus calls Him:
        Counselor (as in "counselor"-at-law)—
            Revised Standard Version;
        Comforter (not a warm, comforting
                "security blanket"
              but from the Latin *conforiare,*
              "to strengthen much"), thus
        Strengthener—King James Version;
        Advocate—The New English Bible;
        Helper—The New American Standard Version.
  Other terms are
                Intercessor,
                Supporter,
                Standby.
The Greek word *parakletos* is evidently difficult
to translate with one word. It refers only to
        "one who is called upon to help another,
          to intercede in behalf of another."
Although it may be hard to find the best
                English translation—
      it is not hard to understand the meaning!

Jesus tells us that the Holy Spirit is
                              on our side,
                              by our side!
        He is not "out there" somewhere,
                    "over against" us—
                              He is here,
                                  where we are,
                                        for us.
                    He is on the same side we are!

Something like that happens in a marriage.
      Two people come out from all other people,
                    stand side by side,
                    on the same side,
        and promise always to remain on the same side.
                    Sometimes when Mary Jo and I
                         are "discussing"—which
              is a much better term than "fussing,"
              one of us will say to the other,
              "Whose side are you on, anyhow?"
There is no question about whose side the Holy Spirit
    is on!
                         Can we really hear that?
                         Can we really believe it?

The only other term Jesus uses for the Spirit is the
                    "Spirit of truth."
              There is no translation problem here!
                    He is the Spirit of truth.
I think of the familiar words in I John:
              God is light,
              and in him is no darkness at all.
                    (1:5)

In God there is no caprice, no deceit, no trickery—
                    and His Spirit is the Spirit of truth.

His Spirit will not lead us into falsehood nor darkness.
                    He is the Spirit of truth.
His Spirit is not the Spirit of emotion nor of ecstasy.
                    He is the Spirit of truth
                              by our side,
                              on our side.

What does Jesus say about the *ministry* of the Spirit?
    As I read and reflect on these sayings of Jesus,
    I see the Spirit's ministry as being one of
                              presence.

    The Holy Spirit is
    God's personal,
          present presence

                    with us—here and now.
                    God revealed in Jesus,
                  actively, personally present
              in power *now*.
    A good, short, non-theological
      definition of the Holy Spirit is

                              God in action.
          Wherever God goes, the Holy Spirit goes.
          Whatever God does, the Holy Spirit does.
          Where the Spirit is, there God is.
                    Because the Spirit is *God in action!*

It's easy for us to separate the Holy Spirit
                              from God,
                          isn't it?
          Oh, we think of Him as divine,
          but we isolate Him and think of Him

                                    separately.
In fact, I have come to believe that, generally,
    we are *tri-theists* instead of *trinitarians.*
    How's that for a profound remark?

What I really mean is:
>>at the practical level,
>we believe in three Gods,
>>side by side,
>instead of one God
>>whose nature it is to be a fellowship.

We don't think we have three Gods—

>>>>but *I* think we do.
>>>*And I think I'm right!*

There is God, the Father.
>He is the Creator God who made us,
>>gave us the Ten Commandments,
>>>and will pronounce judgment on us.

There is Jesus, the Son.
>He is the Savior God who loved/loves us,
>>gave us the Sermon on the Mount,
>>>and died for us.

There is the Holy Spirit.
>He is the Spirit God
>>who fills us
>>>or zaps us
>>>>or baptizes us
>>>>>or does whatever it is
>>>>>>He does to us!

I think when we think of God in this way,
>we end up—not with one God—but with three
>>who sometimes seem scarcely related!
>(We may even have a problem knowing which one
>>to pray to
>>>without hurting the other Ones' feelings!)

Unfortunately, when we think this way,
>we also end up
>>>with three Bibles
>>>and three religious experiences!

The Father God's Bible
   is the Old Testament,
      and the religious experience is condemnation.
The Jesus God's Bible
  is the New Testament Gospels,
    and the religious experience is forgiveness
         and new birth.
The Holy Spirit God's Bible
  is Acts and the Epistles,
    and the religious experience is sanctification
        or the Spirit-filled life
        or Spirit baptism.
    Three Gods—side by side!

        But we don't believe in three Gods.
          We believe in one God!
       We really aren't *tri-theists.*
      We are *trinitarians.*
This means that in the unity of God
there is the manifestation of a kind
of "threeness" which does not mean
    three
     separate
     entities,
    but *oneness* expressed in holy fellowship.

When we speak of the Father,
  we are not speaking of someone
      separate from God.
    We are thinking of God in
      a certain way!
When we speak of God, the Son,
  we are thinking of God in His self-revelation,
      the incarnate Lord Jesus.

When we speak of the Holy Spirit,
we are thinking of
God revealed in Jesus
now *present* among us,
in love and in power.
These are three manifestations,
three personal expressions
of the one Sovereign God
whom we know as
Father,
Son, and
Holy Spirit.
Well, this isn't a lesson on the Trinity.
Rather, *it is a call to get our Gods together!*

The Christian life means many beautiful things
to many people.
For me, personally,
the most beautiful
is the privilege of
personal fellowship with God!
That fellowship is mine and yours
through the ministry of His own Spirit.
Jesus indicated to His disciples that
the Holy Spirit would be to them
all that His own personal presence was—
and more!
We have the privilege of that fellowship, too,
through the Spirit's ministry of *presence.*

Jesus also said that the Spirit
has a ministry of *guidance.*
He will teach you all things, and
bring to your remembrance all that
I have said to you. (14:26)

As we respond to the Holy Spirit,
        He becomes our Teacher.

             We need one, don't we?
I thank God you don't have to be smart
    to be a Christian!

            That lets me in!
      On the other hand,
        it's no special blessing to be dumb.

When you think about it,
   we are about as dumb as we can be
     and still get by!
        Especially we American activist types!
   We have no time to reflect,
          to meditate,
          to think things through.
     We have time only
      to run around
    and keep busy
   and fill our lives with noise!

We don't even know what we believe!
   When problems come along that we can't handle,
   we fuss and stew and take an aspirin.
        Or we lie down and take a nap
          and hope it will pass!
When we are confronted with
   strange doctrines
   and a hundred Bible verses

          out of context,
      we get shook up and run to the
      pastor, crying,
      "What do we believe?"
      (You know, God can forgive sin,
    but what can He do with stupidity?)

If we will let Him,
    He will be our Teacher.
If we will listen,
    He will send His own Spirit to be our Guide.
Jesus said
    that His Spirit would teach us His words.
                                    His words.
    (If you have read this far in the book, you know
                that I believe that Christians
            like you and me—especially
        those of us who are concerned
        about life in the Spirit—
    do not take as seriously as we ought
    the words of Jesus.)
We are just not sure how they fit
    into our life in the Spirit.
                    And I'm wondering why that is so.
Perhaps it goes back to the way
    we think of God—
        or rather, our three Gods.
You see, if we have an Old Testament Father God
                who condemns us,
    and a New Testament Gospels Jesus
                who loves us and saves us,
and an Acts and Epistles Holy Spirit
            who fills and empowers us,
                where do the words of Jesus fit in?
Perhaps it relates to the way
    our Bible is put together—
    or the way we read it.
    We pass from
            condemnation in the Old Testament,
            to grace and salvation in the Gospels,
            to fullness of the Spirit in
                        Acts and the Epistles.

Now we know that the "native land"
of life in the Spirit
is Acts and the Epistles.
But the question remains:
Where do the words of Jesus fit in?

There is a tremendous ground swell of concern
about life and the Spirit,
about the gifts of the Spirit,
about the ministries within the church.
So we read Acts and I Corinthians and Ephesians,
and the words of Jesus
are "back there" somewhere—
unheard and unremembered.

Let me illustrate:
A friend of mine was preaching
a series of sermons on Sunday mornings
from the Sermon on the Mount.
After a few weeks, one of the dear brothers
of the church came to talk to him. He was
greatly distressed because the pastor was
not preaching "holiness."

When my friend told me about it,
I thought, "How awful!
How can you preach the words of Jesus
and *not* preach holiness?!"

But I understand the brother's feelings
even while I don't agree with them.
He wanted his pastor to preach the Bible call
to a holy life.
He simply had categories that did not
include the words of Jesus:

A sermon on Pentecost   Yes.
I Thessalonians 5:23   Yes.
Hebrews 9:13,14   Amen!
I Corinthians 13   Great!
Sermon on the Mount   *What?!*
   (That sermon was before the
Holy Spirit came at Pentecost!)

I think this dear brother is not the only one
                              with this problem.
Just how do the words of Jesus
      relate to the ministry of the Holy Spirit
                                    in our lives?
   Jesus Himself gave us the answer if we will hear it!
                     It is the ministry of the Spirit
                     to bring to our remembrance—
                     that is, our observance—
                     the words that Jesus spoke.
Jesus' words are not back there
obsoleted by the coming of the Spirit!
                          They are out in front of us!
      In fact, the words of Jesus are preserved in
                          Matthew,
                          Mark,
                          Luke, and
                          John precisely because
            the early church, filled with the Spirit,
            remembered the words of Jesus
         and talked about the things He had done.
   In the years between the resurrection
                  and the writing of the Gospels—
                     thirty to sixty years—
   those Spirit-filled Christians were
      sharing the parables,
         rehearsing the miracles,
            remembering the narratives.

They were
        memorizing them,
        teaching them,
        preaching them,
        catechizing them,
        using them on their evangelistic circuits,
        and were meeting and resolving their
                church problems with them!
        When, by the Spirit,
                Matthew, Mark, Luke, and John
                    were ready to write—
                the materials were there
                all around them
        in the memory and life of the church.

I know that we can't reverse history,
    but I wish we could make one change in our Bibles:
      I wish we could take these four Gospels,
        lift them out of the front of the
                New Testament,
        and place them down around Hebrews
          somewhere.
          Chronologically, that's about where
                they belong.

The Holy Spirit has a guiding ministry,
    and His instruments of guidance are the words of
                Jesus.
      When I read the words of Jesus, they are for me,
                now!

When Jesus says,
        Blessed are the poor in spirit,
          the Holy Spirit says to me, "Down, Boy!"
                I need that.

When Jesus says,
>> **Judge not,**
>>>> the Holy Spirit says, "Back off."
>>>>> *I need that.*

When Jesus says,
>> **Forgive your brother,**
>>>> the Holy Spirit reminds me that
>>>>> *I need that.*

And when Jesus says,
>> **No lustful look,**
>>>> the Holy Spirit reminds me that
>>>>> *you need that!*

The words of Jesus become
>>>> the stuff,
>>>> the material,
>>>> the data
>>>>> used by the Spirit
>>> at the growing edge of my life in Him.
>> I'm not trying to compare the words of Jesus
>>> with the words of Paul,
>>> or to say that the Gospel of John is better
> than the Epistle to James.
What I'm saying—saying because I am hearing—
> is that the words of Jesus are for us!
>>>>> They are for us
>>>>> here and now
>>> as we seek to live life in the Spirit.
I'm remembering that in all the sayings of Jesus
regarding the ministry of the Holy Spirit
>> there was only one word about receiving Him
>> and remaining in His "forever" fellowship:
>>> **If you love me, you will keep my**
>>> **commandments.**
>>> **And I will pray the Father,**
>>> **and He will give you another Counselor,**
>>>>> **to be with you for ever.**

The chapter is getting too long—
let's bring it together with this final word of Jesus
about the Spirit:

He will glorify me. (16:14)

The Holy Spirit also has a ministry of exaltation.
He lifts up the lifted-up Jesus.
He exalts the exalted Christ.
Jesus gives content to our conception of the Father:
What is God like?
He is like Jesus!
He also gives content to our idea of the Holy Spirit.
What is the Holy Spirit like?
He is like Jesus!
And His ministry is to glorify Jesus.
By His personal presence
and by His guidance,
He places Jesus
at the center of our lives!

Oh Jesus,
we thank you for your Holy Spirit,
the Spirit of truth
who is by our side
and on our side.
We thank you that through Him
your presence is real to us.
We open our hearts to the Spirit:
Is there some new word we need to hear from you?
Don't let us close our hearts and minds to the Spirit
because of false ideas or bad mental images.
Spirit of our living Christ,
teach us,
guide us,
bring home to our hearts
the words of our Lord,
and give us grace to obey.
Amen.

Chapter Seven
I AM WHO I AM
(John 17:6-26)

What is your name, Lord? A girl named Faith; A guy named Reuben; The Great "I AM!"

Chapter 7

When Jesus was on earth,
    He came to us from God.
        He did the works of God,
           and spoke to us on behalf of God.
Jesus also came from *us*.
    He did what we do,
        talked like we talk,
           and spoke to God on our behalf!

I think the most beautiful example of this is found
    in Jesus' prayer as recorded in the seventeenth
           chapter of John.
    It is called the High Priestly Prayer
  because, in it,
        The One who *comes* from God
           prepares to *go* to God.
        The One who spoke the Father's words to us
           prays to the Father *about* us.
        The One who brought God to where we are
        brings us to where God is!

Jesus fulfills the unique role
of a priest
in this prayer.
He brings God to us
and brings us to God.

This is a
formal,
stylized,
incredibly beautiful
prayer
that seems to gather up
all the major themes of
Jesus' life and ministry
as written in John's Gospel.

Perhaps it would be good to review the setting.
Remember, it is late, late Thursday night
before Jesus' death on Good Friday.
He is with the eleven who represent
the infant Church.
The words He spoke that night reveal
His understanding of Himself,
His understanding of His disciples,
and His concern for His Church.

They are the words of the incarnate Lord
to His infant Church
on the eve of His death.
They are the words of the risen Lord
to His growing Church
at the time of their writing by the old Apostle.
They are the words of our interceding Priest
to His abiding Church
today, tomorrow, and forever!
Let's read these words together:

"I have manifested thy name to the men whom thou gavest me out of the world; thine they were, and thou gavest them to me, and they have kept thy word. Now they know that everything that thou hast given me is from thee; for I have given them the words which thou gavest me, and they have received them and know in truth that I came from thee; and they have believed that thou didst send me.

"I am praying for them; I am not praying for the world but for those whom thou hast given me, for they are thine; all mine are thine, and thine are mine, and I am glorified in them. And now I am no more in the world, but they are in the world, and I am coming to thee. Holy Father, keep them in thy name, which thou hast given me, that they may be one, even as we are one. While I was with them, I kept them in thy name, which thou hast given me; I have guarded them, and none of them is lost but the son of perdition, that the scripture might be fulfilled. But now I am coming to thee; and these things I speak in the world, that they may have my joy fulfilled in themselves.

"I have given them thy word; and the world has hated them because they are not of the world, even as I am not of the world. I do not pray that thou shouldst take them out of the world, but that thou shouldst keep them from the evil one. They are not of the world, even as I am not of the world. Sanctify them in the truth; thy word is truth. As thou didst send me into the world, so I have sent them into the world. And for their sake I consecrate myself, that they also may be consecrated in truth.

"I do not pray for these only, but also for those who believe in me through their word, that they may all be one; even as thou, Father, art in me, and I in thee, that they also may be in us, so that the world may believe that thou hast sent me. The glory which thou hast

given me I have given to them, that they may be one
even as we are one, I in them and thou in me, that
they may become perfectly one, so that the world
may know that thou hast sent me and hast loved
them even as thou hast loved me.
"Father, I desire that they also, whom thou hast
given me, may be with me where I am, to behold my
glory which thou hast given me in thy love for me
before the foundation of the world. O righteous
Father, the world has not known thee, but I have
known thee; and these know that thou hast sent me.
I made known to them thy name, and I will make it
known, that the love with which thou hast loved me
may be in them, and I in them."

(John 17:6-26)

I feel like saying,
"In Jesus' name, Amen."

In this magnificent prayer,
Jesus shares with His Father
the things He has accomplished during His
earthly time.

I have manifested thy name to the men
whom thou gavest me out of the world.
I have made known to them thy name,
and I will make it known.
(vv. 6, 26)

Jesus gives us God's name.

Today names generally don't have a lot
of what we would call *prophetic significance.*
(That is, our names do not say anything
special about us.)

I know a girl named Faith,
but she is not any more trusting
than a Karen or a Debbie.
When our first daughter was born,
we named her Pamela Ann.
(As I think about it now, I'm not really sure why.)
It just seemed like a good name
at the time.
My name is Reuben.
Along with myself, others have at times
wondered why!
I was born way out in the country
in the front bedroom
of a farmhouse.
My grandfather was back east preaching.
Everybody called him "Uncle Buddy,"
but his real name was Reuben.
I have been told that when he heard I had arrived,
he sent my mother a money order for $50, and
she named me Reuben!
I haven't had any problems with that name
from that time to this,
because I understand perfectly
why I am named Reuben.
And if you had sent me
a check for $50
when my first girl was born,
I would have named her after you!

A biblical name is not just a label of identification.
It is an expression of the essential nature
of the person who bears the name.
A person's name
reveals his character.

Esau says of his deceiving brother,
Is he not rightly named *Jacob?*
For he has supplanted me these
two times. (Genesis 27:36)
The name *Jacob* in the Old Testament
means "one who takes by the heel."
After twenty years of deception and fraud, Jacob
met God at Peniel.
In the soul-deep struggle
of a wrestling match,
the man of God said to him,
What is your name? and he replied,
Jacob. Then he said, Your name shall
no longer be called Jacob, but *Israel*
(one who prevails with God).
(Genesis 32:28)
The name reflects the character,
and when the character is changed,
the name is changed!
Aren't you glad
that we aren't stuck
with whatever our names happen to mean?
Real changes can take place.
We are not bound to old names,
old terms,
old ways.
God has promised us a new name.
You shall be called by a new name
which the mouth of the Lord will give.
(Isaiah 62:2)

What about God's name?
The name of God stands for His character.
To know the name of God is to know Him.
His name reveals to us the way He wants to be
known.
The name and the person go together.

You shall not take the name
of the Lord your God in vain.
(Exodus 20:7)
"To take the name in vain" is to
dishonor the person of God.
Our Father who art in heaven,
hallowed be thy name.
(Matthew 6:9)
To *"hallow the name" is to*
reverence the Father.
When we communicate the name of God,
we are not transmitting a
secret,
magic,
power-filled word
that changes things when spoken.
We know that God revealed Himself
to Israel by the name "Jehovah"
or "Yahweh"
which may be translated:
I am who I am.
I am because I am.
I will be what I will be.
I cause to be what exists.
What does that mean?
Hard to know, exactly.

Perhaps it is intentional,
for the mystery of God is not captured in a term,
but in the way He makes Himself known through
His acts.

He is, indeed, what He is
and truly accomplishes what He says.

From the time of Moses,
the Israelites knew God
by His Jehovah-Yahweh name—
the great *I Am.*

As time went on,
the sacredness of the name
was emphasized more and more,
until it was no longer pronounced—
even in worship.

And then Jesus came!
Jesus, the incarnate *I Am*
broke the silence
and spoke the name of God
through His giving,
loving,
surrendered life.
Jesus came among us not only *knowing* the name of God
but *bearing* the name of God.
He is the ultimate revelation of God to His people.
In the Old Testament God instructed His people
to worship at the place where He put His name—
at the Tabernacle and
in the Temple.
Jesus' own person replaces the Tabernacle/Temple!
He is the promise of God's presence.
He is the place where we meet God!
He is the place where God has put His name!

Have you ever wandered out under the stars
in a moment of deep longing and loneliness,
feeling the reality of human weakness, and cried,
"God, who are you? What is your name?"

The answer to that question is not a term or a label.
And if, in response to the cry of existential anguish,
a deep, holy voice would answer,
"I am Jehovah!"
(or "Yahweh" if you've been to the seminary!)
I think, through our tears, we would say,
"Please, God, that's not what I had in mind."

Well, we do cry out, in one way or another:
            "God, who are you?
            What is your name?"
            And that heart-cry, thank God,
            is answered in the lived-out life of Jesus.
                He has given us God's name.
                He has shown us the Father.

God knows me.
He knows me by my Reuben name.
He calls me by my name.
            He knows you by your very own name.
            He also tells us His name.
                So we know each other!
                He is the Jesus-God.

Oh God,
    Sometimes, like Philip, we say,
            "Show us the Father."
    And sometimes we cry out,
            "Who are you, God?
            What is your name?"
        You know the heart hunger that prompts that cry.
        In the midst of the mystery that is our life,
        we must have more than names—
                we want to know who you are,
                    where you are.
                We want to call you by name!
    We thank you, we praise you
        that you have revealed yourself to us
        through our Lord Jesus.
        You are the Christlike God who knows our names.
        We are your people who know your name—
                the real you.
            You come to us in Jesus.
            We thank you.
            Amen.

Chapter Eight
GIVE ME YOUR GLORIES

(John 17—Selected verses)

Eavesdropping; Pianos, football players, and potluck suppers; Can you play the ukelele? Spirit gifts.

Chapter 8

Part of the wonder of the Priestly Prayer of John 17
    is that we are privileged to overhear Jesus
       as He talks to His Father about Himself.
In the last chapter we heard Him say:
    I have manifested thy name.
    I have made known to them thy name.
        (v. 6)

In this one let's listen to another word
    our Lord speaks about Himself.
     It is the beautiful word *glory*.
    All mine are thine, and thine are mine,
    and I am glorified in them . . .
    The glory which thou hast given me
    I have given them, that they may be one
    even as we are one . . .
    Father, I desire that they also,
    whom thou hast given me,
        may be with me where I am,
    to behold my glory which thou hast given me
    in thy love for me
        before the foundation of the world.
        (vv. 10, 22, 24)

Jesus gives us God's name.
Jesus shows us God's glory.

I've been thinking about the word *glory*
and have concluded that I don't know much about it.
Most of what I know
about glory
is that I want some!
I've heard the old-timers exhort:
"Get under the spout
where the glory comes out!"
Well, whoever is controlling
the spigot, let me know!
I want some!

The word *glory* is used in the Bible to refer
to those encounters of the divine and the human
when the presence of God meets the earthly scene.
His presence is somehow made known,
made visible,
manifested.
When God appears in a bush that burns
but is not consumed,
there is glory!
When God encounters Moses, His man
on the mountain,
there is glory!
When God meets His people anywhere,
under any circumstances,
there is glory!

Now the word *glory* is a fascinating word.
In the Old Testament it is a word that
carries with it the idea of "weight" or "substance."
In the New Testament,
Paul speaks of an "eternal weight of glory."

In the Old Testament the word used as "weight" or
"substance" referred to that which a person
possessed,
>causing others to give him reverence or respect.
>In biblical times people who were "portly"
>>*(Isn't that a kind*
>>*way to say it?)*
were those who had enough money to buy the food
>to become portly!
>So you might say
>that a portly person
carried a lot of weight in the community!

Now it isn't hard to see how that meaning
>could move from "substance" or "weight" to
>>influence and
>>respect and
>>value and
>>meaning and
>>reality and
>>clout!
>>A person's glory as we are now using it
>>is that which gives his or her life
>>>influence and
>>>respect and
>>>value and
>>>meaning and
>>>reality and
>>>*clout!*

Glory also seems to carry with it the idea of shining.
>A good synonym for glory, then, would be
>*radiance.*
>>It's an observable phenomenon, isn't it?
>>>In the traditional wedding write-ups,
>>>brides are usually described as *radiant.*

That term is never used of the groom.
He may be "wishing he were in Scotland,
fishing tonight!" But the bride is *radiant!*
Now, I don't know how to define that,
but you can tell it when you see it, can't you?
In my old age, I am getting bolder
than I used to be about asking
young couples how they are getting along.
"How are you doing?"
"How is married life?"
"Do you still love her/him?"
"Are you still speaking?"
"Are you getting along all right?"
But I'm finding out that I don't
really have to ask those questions
to gather information. I can tell
by looking at people how they are getting along!
What is it that gives our lives the radiance,
the joy,
the lift,
the light?
*This is enough of a definition
for me to want some!*

Jesus said,
**The glory which thou hast given me
I have given them, that they may be one
even as we are one.**

I've been around school long enough to observe
that every September a new crop of freshmen
arrive, bearing their glories with them!
*(You know, all the local
"teen talent" winners who are
going to take the campus by storm?)*
So, at the first parties and get-togethers,
"x" number of people always gather around the piano
and shove each other off the bench doing their thing.

There are the singers
and the players
and the guitar pickers.

And, of course, there are
the local high school super jocks!
And the eggheads, too!

It's really funny how we tend
to show off our "glories" at such times!
I don't know whether
to laugh or cry.
Because during those first few days,
there is a kind of shuffling of glories.
And, at the parties, those who do a lot of
laughing
sometimes go back to their rooms to cry
because their glories have been
shuffled
and their identities have been
threatened.

Run this back to your local church
for a minute.
There are the people whose glory lies in
their ability to play the piano or the organ.
If you don't believe it, try to get them off the bench!
There are people in my age bracket
whose glory is their grandchildren—
and all you have to do is say Hello!
and out comes the billfold and all the pictures!
There are the ladies in your home church
whose glory is in their cooking expertise.
They can hardly wait for the next potluck supper!
(They're the ones who bring the dishes that
everybody has to have some of!)
That's their glory!
What's yours?

Some of you know all the names
  of all the football players
    on all the major league teams.   *That's your thing.*
Some people glory in their clothes and wardrobes.
  They shop only at Jacque Penet— *downtown branch!*
                  I know some preachers
                    whose glory is in their books.
              The books serve roughly the same
              purpose as wallpaper—only thicker.
I wish I hadn't talked about that.
I've read the first ten pages of
    more books than you can think of.
                    Once, I even finished one!

What's your glory?
    I've wondered for a long time about the meaning of
      this message from Jesus:
          The glory which thou hast given me
          I have given them, that they may be one
              even as we are one.
As I think about this verse,
    I have begun to discover a strange dichotomy.
    On the one hand, our glory is that which gives us
        meaning and
        weight and
        substance and
        value and
        worth and
        radiance and
        clout.
                  On the other hand,
                   those are the very things
                  that divide
              and fragment
            and separate us.
                  You know why?
             Because our glory becomes our turf.

Don't ask me to define that term.
All I know is that when I'm on my turf,
and the opposition gets a little close,
I become defensive.

There is an awesome word of Jesus in John 5:44:
How can you believe, who receive
glory from one another and do not seek
the glory that comes from the only God?
Think about that.
It's a fascinating set of dynamics.
You see, if I'm a red-hot ukelele player (and I am!),
and nobody knows about it,
then how will I get my clout?
But if I perform and
you happen to be a
better ukelele player,
I am threatened
and this separates
and divides us.

Jesus said,
The glory which thou has given me . . .
What was Jesus' glory?
What was it that gave Him His
meaning and
value and
authority and
confidence and
radiance?
I don't get the feeling that His glory
was in what He wore.
Foxes have holes, and
the birds of the air have nests;
but the Son of man has nowhere to
lay his head.
(Matthew 8:20)

He had some good people around Him, but
I doubt that His clout was in His ability
to direct and choose personnel.
One of His followers betrayed Him
and one of them denied him,
and the whole bunch took off under pressure.
(Individually, they weren't anything special.)

I know that He was a great preacher-teacher and,
if I know anything about that at all, I'm sure
there was a sense of joy and fulfillment in sharing.
Yet during the most popular phase
of His ministry,
there was an underlying deep disappointment
because the people weren't
seeing what there was to see or
hearing what there was to hear.

Wherein, then, was Jesus' glory?
I have come to believe that it was in
His total dependency upon His Father.
Throughout His life, He said,
I came not to do my own will,
but the will of my Father.
The words that I say I don't say of myself
but of the Father who dwells in me
and does His work.
What I do I do not of myself.
I do not seek the glory that comes from men.
Jesus' glory was in the totality of
His dependence upon His Father,
His obedience to His Father,
His utter trust in His Father,
His profound awareness that
in all the affairs of life,
His Father was in control.

Now what I am thinking is that
    if my glory is something I can *do*,
        that's really fine until somebody comes along
                        who can do it better!
    If my glory is in who I *know,* who I cotton to,
        then I am dependent upon those people
                      who might let me down!
So I live defensively,
with tension and stress and fear.
But if I yield my glories to God,
   so that what gives me my sense of worth and value
      is not what I can do
           or what I have
              or who I know—
                        if my glory is in my
                        relationship
                    with my Father—
              my total dependence upon Him—
then when someone comes along who has more
books than I have,
    or who has read more of them,
        or who can preach better than I can—
                it doesn't hurt quite as much
                        for quite as long!
I think that's what makes it possible in part
    for us to maintain the unity of the Spirit
        in the bond of peace
           amidst the diversity of gifts from the Body.

Consider the matter of gifts and ministries.
    Perhaps many people would have
        a more benevolent
        attitude toward the gifts thing
           and the charismatic thing
           and the tongues thing
                if they were not so divisive!

That's one of my own personal hassles about it,
and, naturally, I see myself to be a person of
understanding and
tolerance and
acceptance!
I just wish these things were not so divisive!

Isn't it weird that, seemingly, the very gifts of the Spirit
intended to make it possible for us
to be what we are, and
do what we do, and
develop unity in the body
are the things that
so easily divide us?
Maybe it's because there is a subtle shift from
total dependence upon God to dependence
upon the gift
so that my value,
meaning,
worth,
radiance,
clout
are found not in
what I can do, or
what God has done for me.

Jesus' glory was tied to the depths
of His surrender to His Father.
When the crowds flattered Him,
He didn't lose His poise.
When they rejected Him,
He didn't lose His nerve.
When they crucified Him,
He didn't lose His love!
Somewhere in here, folks,
there is a cross!

Of course there is a fundamental human need
   for self-worth and meaning.
     Everyone needs to be able to do something.
                    *I hope you can
                     do something.*
    It's terrible to grow up feeling like:
          "I can't do anything."
          "I ain't nobody."
          "Nobody cares."
             That's a bummer
               all the way.
    I know and recognize the need for
     a sense of self-worth and
            self-confidence and
             self-acceptance.
It's just that when those things become
the basis of our being,
the ground of our glory,
it's all up for grabs!

But if I take my glories to the cross,
    I can use them or not use them
      without being personally destroyed
       and without dividing the body.
             *I'm hearing some words
              right now.*
*The message is
loud and clear.*
      God forbid that I should glory
      Save in the cross of our Lord Jesus Christ!

Father,
    *what is my glory?
     Don't let me back away
      from that probing question.*

Am I finding my meaning
             and value
             and self-worth
                in something other than you?
             I give my little glories to you.
             Let your glory become my glory.

Father,
        are there some reading these words who are saying,
                    "I don't have any glory."
                    "I can't do anything."
                "I don't have any gift that is worthwhile."
                "I don't even know what radiance means!"
Please may they find their worth in you,
                        their meaning in your love,
                            their purpose in your will,
                                their radiance in your
                                        fellowship.

        *In your name—and for your **glory.***
                            Amen.

Chapter Nine
HUNGER TO BE HOLY
(John 17—Selected verses)

Missing persons; It's hard to be holy with the television on! A time for tension; "Holification" and "sanct"; God-people.

Chapter 9

In the Priestly Prayer
the thoughts of Jesus go far beyond Himself.
We hear Him share with His Father
His concerns for those of us
who are His disciples.

Jesus prayed *about* us
and prayed *for* us
on that awesome night.
Read again with me these words:
**I am not praying for the world but
for those whom thou hast given me,
for *they are thine*. (17:9)**
We belong to God!

May I ask you a very personal question?
To whom do you really belong?
That's a good question, isn't it?
To whom are you fully present?

126

Have you ever tried to characterize
  those times of your life
    when you were fully present
      to something or someone?
        Have you ever felt, in the midst of conversation,
          that you were really "missing"?
            That your mind and heart were
                somewhere else?

There are students in our school
  who may have registered in September,
      but who *have never been present!*
        Their bodies are here,
      and they report to class,
    and do "x" numbers of things
    at the ends of their pencils,
    but they are "absent"!
  Where are we when we are altogether,
            totally present?
I think we instinctively know that we belong to God
          ultimately,
        and that where we
         need to be
      is in His presence!
Disciples belong to God.
  That really settles the matter of ownership,
    doesn't it?
    But are we fully present in His fellowship, or
        are we "missing persons"?

Then Jesus said another thing that fascinates me. He
  said,
      They are in the world.

      Well, of course they are in the world, Lord.
          Where else?
        I wonder why He said that?

And now I am no more in the world, but they are
in the world, and I am coming to thee . . .
I do not pray that thou shouldst
take them out of the world, but
that thou shouldst keep them
from the evil one.
(vv. 11, 15)

That statement has been helping me.
   I think many of us have a kind of
      built-in understanding
        that true discipleship or holy living should be
         lived out in an unreal world.
I think we think that if we really were as
    holy or as disciplined or as committed as
                        we ought to be,
               our lives would be out of this world!
But there is an insight for us!
   Jesus didn't pray that we be taken out of the world!
               I know what the song says:
          This world is not my home,
          I'm just a passing thru,
          My treasures are laid up
          Somewhere beyond the blue.
                Outside of not being true,
                 it's not a bad song!
Many of the songs we sing,
       sermons we've heard,
         ways of thinking that have been passed
                  down
             through the generations
       communicate essentially this same truth:
     We don't really belong in this world.
         But Jesus says we do!
I know I am just passing through,
but *this world is still my home!*

Many of us have developed the "if only" syndrome.
I have the feeling that "if" things were "only" different
in my world . . .
I know, for instance, that I could be a better Christian
if my house were arranged differently.
Now the way my house is—there is a living room
and then we have a den with a sliding glass door.
The living room is the room
where the good light is,
and the good chairs are,
so that you can just sit,
and read the Bible,
and meditate
and be holy.

But the trouble is, just down the way in the den
is the television set
where my two "deaf" children watch.
It's hard to be holy in the living room when
just over there the television is playing
and, besides that, it sounds so
interesting
sometimes.
You understand, I don't like
television,
but, occasionally, I have to check and
see what's going on, and I get there
just in time to see some dastardly deed
done to a fellow primate, and I say,
"Well, how come that?"
So one hour and forty-seven commercials later,
I'm not as holy as I was before!
The house is just not set up for me to be holy in.
I guess I could go be holy in the kitchen,
but the refrigerator is there.
Or I could go be holy in the bedroom,
but the bed is there.

(Did you ever kneel down to pray and wake up
with your feet gone sound asleep? And
a crick in your neck?)
I never do know whether to play like
it didn't happen,
or ask the Lord to forgive me!
What I need is another room added on to our house
for me to be holy in—
but Mary Jo would put the sewing machine in there!

I could be more holy if I didn't have
to drive the freeway to work!
I kid you not!
Day by day, I
set out from home to go be
a blessing at school, and by the
time I get there,
I need prayers!
I leave home at a quarter of seven in the morning,
and the freeway is already full of
dumbhead people
who crowd the lanes and give stupid signals!
You understand me, don't you?

I could be more holy if my dog would die.
(Is it moral to pray for your dog to die?)
But I'm too nice to do that,
and besides,
the rest of the family is praying on the other side!

I could be a better Christian if people
would leave me alone at school.
(Don't call me, I'll call you!")

During the years that I have been chaplain, I have
wanted to put up a sign that said:
I'm your friendly, loving chaplain.
Tuesdays and Thursdays, 2:00 to 4:00.
or
Do not Disturb.
Being Holy!

I wrote a book entitled *We Really Do Need Each Other*
and
I'm working on a sequel,
WILL EVERYBODY PLEASE LEAVE ME ALONE!

You could be more holy
if you had a different roommate,
if you had a better car—or even a car!
if you had a different job,
if your spouse were different,
if your house were different—
If . . . if . . . if . . .
For too long, the basic presuppositions of my
life
have been these kinds of things,
every one of which is fundamental to our life
in this world!
Home
Family
Pets
TV
Work
People
Car
These are the things that the common life
is made of!

I have begun to see that the "if only" syndrome leads to
isolation
and exclusiveness,
a rejection of the created world,
a turning away from God's order.
This kind of thinking superimposes upon
the naturalness of life
a kind of super spirituality
that denies the validity of our
existence.
But this world is still our home!

We're not going to be here forever,
but, in the meantime,
did you know that we live here?
We have ears to hear with and sounds to hear.
We have feet to walk with and places to go.
We have lungs to breathe with and, so far,
there is still some unpolluted air to breathe.
We have arms to hug with and people who need
our love.
We have hearts to care with and people who need
our care.
We have lips to speak with and words to be said.
And
if we didn't know better,
you would think we were made to be here.

Jesus said,

They are in the world.
I do not pray that thou shouldst take them
out of the world
but that thou shouldst keep them from the
evil one.

(17:11, 15)

I believe that God's will for us is not so much
to be separated
from the things of the world
as to be separated
from our own false selves—
set free to live in His world and use
His "things" for His glory!

My responsibilities take me out of town
from time to time.
And I have reasonable assurance,
based on the law of averages,
that something will go wrong at home
while I'm away.
I'm reasonably sure that
the dog won't die.
(Don't hate me!
You just don't know my dog!)
I know that my office won't be different
when I get back.
It will just be piled higher with
mail and stuff
that needs to be done.
But whatever goes wrong—
it means everything to me to know that this is my world!

And I hear Jesus saying that what He has for us,
He has for us in this world where we live!
The life that we live in the Lord is indeed
a life of tension.
And the tension is found in the two statements:
They are thine.
and
They are in the world.

Disciples belong to God; but, they are in the world.
I'm not sure that we have really
recognized as deeply as we ought
the ambivalent character of our lives
as we live them "between the times."
We live "between the times" of
the first and second coming,
the time of birth and death,
the time of our entering into life in
Christ
and being made perfect in Him in glory.
In the tensions that are a part of the human existence,
our belonging is to God;
our participation is in the world.
It is not a simple thing to be an obedient disciple
in the world.
I have come to believe
that we have developed
a kind of spiritual religion
that makes me wonder if we aren't
more spiritual than Jesus!
I did not say
"more holy"!

But our religion has a tendency to move toward
spirituality
and away from
the world.
Somehow Jesus was able to keep both
right where they belong.
How was He able to accomplish this?
What is it that our Lord wants for His Church
that is in the world and not of it?
Let me gather some scriptures from this seventeenth
chapter
that at least point us toward the answer:

Sanctify them in the truth; thy word is truth.
As thou didst send me into the world,
so I have sent them into the world.
And for their sake I consecrate myself,
  that they may also be consecrated in truth.
       (vv. 17-19)

The prayer of Jesus for His in-the-world Church
                is that it be holy—
    His heart's desire for us real-world type people
                is that we be holy.

        Now let me talk a little bit about that.
I wish all our English words related to the word *holy*
           had the same sound.
All the Greek words for *holy* have a basic
  sound similarity
      because they come from one Greek word *hagias*.
     I wish, for all the words that cluster around
        the idea of holy,
    that there were a single sound in our language.
For instance, we have the Anglo-Saxon word family
         holy.
      Another word in this family is
        holiness,
      and we ought to have
            holify
        and *holification!*
There is another group of words from the Latin
  word family
    that has an entirely different sound:
        sanctify,
          sanctification,
            sanctity,
        and we need another one
             here—
           sanct!
       I think I like that word.

I really wish we could add these words
  to our vocabulary—
    because I believe that words like
                sanctification
              and
                holiness
              have become technical terms—
            understood only by the initiated.
    These terms are often flown like banners,
        handled as symbols of authority,
              or status symbols.

I may be exaggerating slightly,
  but I perceive that some of these words
    like *sanctification* and *holiness* and *redemption,*
      which at one time were profoundly relevant,
        which were precious and beautiful
                            life-words,
            have, for many people, lost their luster
              and much of their beauty and
                          magnetism.
                Do I make myself clear?
Some of these precious words—these life-words—
        at one time had juice in them;
            they had stuff in them;
            they connoted things;
            they denoted things;
            they were glorious words;
            they were magnetic words.
      But, for many, they have lost something:
        the juice has dried up;
          and they have become technical terms,
            and maybe shibboleths.
                    And, right or wrong,
                        good or bad,
                that is partly true for me as well!

At the same time, I see something else
    going on in the world where I live.
      While some of the old terms have
                            lost their luster,
                    I perceive that there is
                    a growing, deep-heart
                hunger to be holy!
                    I believe that with all my soul!
Maybe this is the hunger to which
  all other hungers are related.
      Maybe this fundamental hunger to be holy
        is that God-shaped vacuum
            in the heart of every person.
                          And, oddly enough,
                      though that hunger persists,
                        it is seldom expressed.
I don't know if we can find
      new terms,
      new language,
      new lingo
        that would help us,
                but I know that there is within us
                      a hunger to be holy.
                  And I know that the heart-hunger
                of our Lord for His Church
            is that the people of God
      be sanctified and
      made meet for the Master's use.

What does it mean to be holy?
I'd like to take the lid off
        on my own journey of understanding.
            It seems to me that at the end of the articles,
                and at the end of the journal studies,
            and at the end of the textbook studies
        on the idea of holiness—one idea emerges:

To be holy means to be different by virtue of
belonging to God.
The first big word in that sentence is the word
  belonging.
You see, only God is holy in any original
    and underived sense. *Only God* in
                His separateness,
                His otherness,
                His purity,
                His wholeness

                                    is holy.
                        Only God is "sanct."

Other things
    or persons
        or places
            become holy by virtue of
            a "holifying" relationship with the God
                            who alone is holy.

That's why the Temple and
            the vessels in the Temple and
            the vestments and
            the oil and
            all the stuff they used in religious ceremonies
                            could be holy—
                        because they belonged to God.
Then what about holy *people?*
Fundamentally, in the Bible, people are holy
                    only because they belong to God.
    In this prayer, Jesus' High Priestly Prayer,
        He asks for our wills,
                    for our hearts
                            to be entirely devoted
                                to God
                            and to His service.

All our talents, all our energies,
all our lives are to be marked
with the seal of consecration.
I think that's the most beautiful
phrase I have heard in a long time—
"marked with the seal of consecration."
This phrase implies the renouncing of self,
just as Jesus was willing to leave heaven and
renounce all heavenly claims.
It means a radical belonging to God!

Look at Israel in the Old Testament.
Israel is nothing apart from
the initiative and the
calling of God.
Into the flow of human history comes Israel,
called into being by God.
I don't know the sources and backgrounds
of other nations, but I do know about Abraham.
I know about Isaac
and Jacob and Joseph.
We know what God said to Moses
on the backslopes of Mt. Horeb.
We know that God brought them out of Egypt
and made them into a nation at the foot of Sinai.
We know that He entered into
covenant relationship with them.
And God said to them:
I didn't call you because
you were beautiful
or because you were wise
or because you were good
or because you were big.
I set my love upon you and
I have called you;
and apart from that calling,
Israel is nothing and has nothing.

Why was it that the prophets kept warning:
     "Don't get involved with Assyria."
     "Don't get involved with Babylon."
     "Don't put your trust in Egypt."
          "Trust God!"
It wasn't because they were political neutralists.
It was because they saw that Israel existed
        for one reason—
      their relationship to God.
    When Israel moved away from
    that fundamental dependency,
     they got into trouble.

It doesn't take a whole lot of brains to
   bring this right over into the New Testament
    and relate
      it to the people of the new covenant,
          the new Israel,
          the Church of God.

    Where does the Church come from?
         We didn't create it.
            God did!
            It's His thing!
He brought it into being in the New Exodus,
    consummated on the cross.
      Liberated by the power of the Spirit,
      we move out under the sign of the cross
      as the new Israel, the people of God.

And God says to us:
    I didn't call you because you were good.
    I didn't call you because you were great.
    I didn't call you because you were anything
     special.

God does not use us because we are

better,
bigger,
richer,
more creative, or
more intelligent.

The Church is what it is because, and only because,
it belongs to God and has been called into existence
by the Word.

And, suddenly, we are right in the middle
of the New Testament ethic that says to us,
"Be what you are."
"Be a God-person."

Jesus said, you remember,
Apart from me, you can do nothing.
To be holy, then, really means
to put at the center of our lives
what is, in fact,
the Center of our lives.
We are to be God-people.

Holiness means God-centeredness.
It means being separated unto Him.
It means belonging to a community
that is the possession of God.

And when we realize that God is intrinsically holy,
we understand why, in the process of moving into
holy relationship with Him, we need
cleansing,
a dying, and
a liberation
from the power
of the carnal mind

And if we are to be persons
in a community which belongs to God,
we also need the empowering of the Holy Spirit.

I am hearing the words
of an old invitation hymn:
Break down every idol,
Cast out every foe.
We are called to be a holy people, a God-people.
And as that word penetrates my life,
I find that it has
increasing power and
increasing beauty and
increasing magnetism and
makes increasing demands and
talks to me about what I say I am—*a God-person.*

The second word in our key sentence is
different.
Different by belonging.
As with old Israel, so with the new Israel.
Old Israel was different from surrounding nations
because every part of its life was related to God.
The people were to reflect His character and will
as spelled out in the Book of the Covenant.

For us of the New Covenant,
it is no different.
Radical belonging issues in lives that
reflect God's character and will.
What does that mean for me personally?

It means my life is to be lived
in growing likeness to Jesus
through the power of His Spirit.
That is the expression of radical belonging!

Jesus said,
Don't take them out of the world.
As thou hast sent me, I have sent them.
Sanctify them through thy truth. Thy word
is truth. As thou hast sent me,
I have sent them.
And for their sake, I sanctify myself that they
may be sanctified in the truth.
When it comes
right down to it,
holiness means *God-centeredness*
Christlikeness,
and *God-sentness.*
And that's the prayer of Jesus
for us.

In the midst of all this,
we are *in* the world,
sent *to* the world.
And if I'm going to be a person that puts God
at the center of my life and proclaims God to the
world,
I'll have to do it with
the rooms of my house arranged the
way they are.
I may have to learn to like the dog!
I may need to learn how to accept
the intrusion of people
around me
to whom I want to shout:
WOULD YOU PLEASE LEAVE ME ALONE
SO I CAN BE HOLY?!

Turn it off!
Take it away!
I want to pray!
No! The word
of the Lord comes to us:
In the world! In the world!
To which, we say, "Yes, Lord!"
I'm sure you are aware that what is on my heart
is really a sharing of some of my own struggles
about what it means to be a holy person, so
it's hard for me to know where this meets

you.

But I want to tell you
that the calling of God
is that we be His people.
We must turn away from
false dependencies and put Him
at the center of our lives!
As our Lord was preparing His people
for His departure,
that yearning cry of His heart to His Father
was that the people He left behind would
be the holy people of God.

I want to be a part of that!
And so do you!
That's our crowd!

Oh God,

the holy God,
the Creator God—
Here we are in our world—
the house,
the job,
the room,
the people,
the things,
the responsibilities.

(Would you stop praying now, and visualize *your*
world—
your home—*your* family—*your* relationships—*your*
places.)

Oh Father, we say **yes** *to our world.*
      Don't let us think we can be more holy
        by leaving it, in fact or in fancy.
We know it is not your will to take us out of it,
      but to enter into it by your Spirit
        in a deeper way than ever before.
                    We open our world to you!
    Break down every idol,
    Cast out every foe.
        We would be your holy people—
          God-centered,
            Christlike,
              and sent to minister
                in the world where we live.
                    Amen.

Chapter Ten
WE ARE TOGETHER

(John 17—Selected verses)

"Mystic sweet communion"; We are cordially invited; Heritage, hobbies, and happy hormones; "Pass the bread."

Chapter 10

I suppose an objective analysis
of the Priestly Prayer
would reveal that it is
"The Prayer of Jesus for the Oneness of His Church."
Over and over again that petition
is heard.
It is the first clear petition for the disciples:

I am praying for them . . .
Holy Father, keep them in thy name,
which thou hast given me,
that they may be one,
even as we are one.
(vv. 9a, 11)

I just want to share what the Lord has been laying
on my heart about these verses.
It is not exactly frightening,
but almost!

> Our priority for oneness
> in the community of believers
> is far lower on our scale of values
> than it was and is for our Lord.

I am coming to believe that oneness in the community
has an extremely high priority for Him
and for the writers in the New Testament.
Oh, if we were listing our priorities,
it would be in there somewhere
if we happened to think about it.

I think most Christians would agree
that oneness is great.
But I'm not sure we
think it is absolutely essential.

But for Jesus
oneness was a vital issue for that infant Church.
And that wasn't all! He included all the rest of us
when He said:
> **I do not pray for these only, but also**
> **for those who are to believe in me**
> **through their word,**
> **that they may *all be one* . . .**
> **that they may become perfectly one,**
> **so that the world may know!**
> **(vv. 20, 23)**

It's almost awesome to me how significant,
how vastly important, is this matter of oneness
in the mind of Jesus.
I've been wondering what it means
to be one,
and I want to share this thought with you.
Oneness in our Lord Jesus Christ
transcends all normal, cultural barriers among us.

Undoubtedly, at one time or another,
  you have sung
the song of the church, one verse of which
  goes like this:

> *Yet she on earth hath union*
> *With God the Three in One,*
> *And mystic sweet communion*
> *With those whose rest is won.*

SAMUEL J. STONE

This means that the church,
  that visible body of Christ, is part of
    all of those
      of all the ages,
        of all the places,
          of all the times,
            who are a part of the blood-washed
                                    body
                    of our Lord Jesus Christ.
                  That means that the oneness
          of which He speaks is
            a oneness
          which encompasses all time.
Just think about that!
            Think of all the cultures.
            Think of all the life-styles.
            Think of all the languages.
              Think of all the different tastes.
        And Jesus prayed: **Make them one!**
                  When I think of all the
                  petty things that separate us,
                      it makes me sick!

I have written about this before,
  but I have the author's permission to repeat it!
I have a mental image I want to share with you.
Will you go with me once more to that upper room
              on that evening of the Last Supper?

Can you see that room?
Can you see Jesus at the head of the table?
Can you see the disciples assembled at their places?
                          In those days, people
                     reclined around the table.
                     I was born too late!

But there they are, the group of twelve,
their elbows on the table in fellowship and intimacy.
     Now I want you to take out the end wall.
          Just take out that wall and lengthen the table.
     Stretch out the table and bring in
          all the Christians of the first century.
                                        Let them come.

Lengthen the table again and invite the Christians
                of the second century to take their places.
                     And let the table grow longer
                               and longer
                                    and longer
                              until it reaches
                         down across the centuries
                         and spans the ages
                          and transcends all space and place
                    until it comes to rest
               right where you are *right now!*

Who is sitting at that table?
All the saints of the ages are there.

                                        Adjust the color.
Can you see the colors of the robes, the hair, the skin?
     Can you see all the shades, all the hues?
          Can you see the costumes, the life-styles?
          Can you see their positions in time?

Now, turn up the audio.
Listen! Can you hear them?
   Listen to the languages.
     Listen to their songs.
       Listen to the sounds of the villages and towns.

Look again!
We are there, sitting with the saints of all the ages!
Why are we there?
               Because we have been invited
             by the Man at the head of the table
                  to share His life.
What are we doing there?
             We're passing the bread—
         the shared, given, broken
        life of Jesus.
        And we are one!

That's what we have in common.
Any talk of the oneness of the Body must be
expressed in that life shared around that table.
All of us know that the Lord's Supper
   is the supreme symbol of the oneness
      of the body of believers, because at that table
        what we share is not
            our commonality,
            our congeniality,
            our common culture,
            our common heritage,
               not our hobbies,
               nor our happy hormones.
                 All that we have in common
                 is the shared life of Jesus—
                    and it's enough.

It's been several years now since
    I had the privilege of becoming chaplain
        of a Christian college.
                And I thought when I came to the college
                    that it would probably be
                heaven on earth
                in terms of oneness.
        Look at all the things students have in common:
                    common age group,
                    common culture,
                    common background,
                    common religious heritage,
                    common socioeconomic status,
                    common ideals and goals.
When you consider all the things that should
bind people together, surely here
we would be one in the Lord!
            But I discovered that in the midst
            of a Christian community of believers,
                there can be
                            loneliness,
                            fragmentation,
                            judgment,
                            separation,
                            status symbols,
                            and divisions
                                that tear it all up.
                            Did you know that?

On the campus of this Christian college,
    after school had been going on for
        three or four weeks,
            there was one girl who had not gone to the
            dining hall yet!
                        She ate her meals out of
                    the vending things in the dormitory!

She was so lonely;
she was so insecure;
she was so bound up;
             she hadn't even gone to the dining hall yet!

I'm sure it wouldn't have blessed her
a whole lot if I had said,
"Your problem is that you're neurotic!"
                              "Oh, thanks! I'll go to the
                                   dining hall now!"
I discovered something else, too.
I found that multiplying activities
doesn't bring oneness, either.
                    In our campus situation we say that
                  if people are lonely and don't get together,
                    we need to have more inter-dorm parties.
Well, we do need more times to get together.
   But the more parties you have for people
   to get together,
        the more occasions there are for
   the lonely people
                    to feel more lonely!
The more dating occasions you have,
the more misery is compounded with the *undating*.
                    I'm coming to see that all of those
superficial things that we think will bring us together
                                                  don't!

                    There is only one thing that will bring us
                              together,
                    and that is our oneness in the Lord!
          That's why I am so concerned and turned on
about groups and Bible studies and prayer fellowships.
If you're having them where you are—good!
Have some more.

                              If not, *why not,*
                    When are you going to start?

We need places to get together
　around the Word,
　　and around the Lord,
　　and around our true oneness.
When we are affirming our true oneness,
　we are, in fact, being what we are—
　　and that's where the loneliness breaks down;
　　　that's where the openness begins;
　　　　　　　that's where the joy is!
　　　　　　　I'm laying this on you
　　　　　　　like you need it,
　　　　　　and I'm just going to assume
　　　　　　　that you do! If you don't—
　　　　well, just praise the Lord *and pass it on!*
I am chagrined at the little things that divide us,
　when, in truth, the oneness that we have in Christ
　　is the great reality within the Christian life.
　　　What I'm seeing like I've never seen before
　　　is that not only must the little things bow,
　　but the biggest things of our lives must bow
　　　　　　　before our oneness in Christ.

Several years ago, my wife and I had the privilege
　of spending some time in Germany, where I spoke
　to an American military congregation in Frankfort.
　Now picture this—
　an American military congregation in Germany:
　　　　　one family from North Dakota,
　　　　　one family from California,
　　　　　one family from Alabama,
　　　　　one family from Oklahoma,
　　　　　one family from Kansas,
　　　　　one family from Michigan—
　　　　　　　each bringing its own perception
　　　　　of what a Nazarene church ought to be.

So they came thinking,
"Well, we're in a strange land, but praise the Lord.
  There are a bunch of good old Nazarenes here!"
                        Lo and behold, when they
                        came together in the church,
            they found other perceptions and other ideas.
And so did we!
  Some wanted old-fashioned, revival preaching,
    and some wanted encounter groups.
  Some wanted "Holy, Holy, Holy"
    and some wanted "Do, Lord!"
  Some wanted a guitar
    and some wanted an organ.
                        And here they all were—
                  coming from the same denomination
                  with all these different expectations.

And you may not believe this,
but this *American* congregation in *Frankfort, Germany*
was pastored by a wonderful, young *Scottish* preacher
who loved his native brogue and who
  pr-r-reached and pr-r-rayed
        for the par-r-rishioner-r-rs of his congregation!
        And the Scottish preacher was married to
      a *German* girl, which meant that the Americans
    couldn't gripe about the Germans because the
  pastor's wife was there!
And, to further complicate things,
  since it was a *military* congregation,
          there was a lieutenant colonel
                    and a sergeant
                on the same church governing board.
        (My guess is that at the board meetings,
        the sergeant would say,
                    "I move we vote by secret ballot!")

There we were—the gathered body of believers.
      And it was a time of some rich insights for me—
        a beautiful time of understanding.
          The Lord began to talk to me about
            some things—
               about oneness and fellowship.
I'm not sure that we were much blessing to that
  wonderful group—
          but they were a blessing to Mary Jo and me!
In that group were all the factors
                  that could divide
                  and separate
                  and alienate
                  the Body.

Instead, there was beautiful fellowship.
At the center of the oneness,
      there was an awareness of the cross on which our
            prejudices,
            expectations,
            anticipations,
            desires
            were nailed for the sake of oneness
               of the life and the Body.
I remembered what St. Paul said:
      There is neither Jew nor Greek,
      there is neither slave nor free,
      there is neither male nor female;
      for you are all one in Christ Jesus.
          (Galatians 3:28)

As I think now about that verse,
  I realize that the oneness of the Body
    is greater than
             prejudice,
             rank,
             sex,

expectations,
anticipations,
nationality!

                                     Nationality.
                                       My soul!
                        That's who we *are!*
Have you ever been to a country where
another language is spoken almost exclusively?
     We were getting along pretty well in Germany.
       I knew a few phrases:
                Auf wiedersehen.
                Entschuldigen Sie!
                      That means "Good-bye"
                      and "Pardon me please!"
But when Mary Jo and I went down to Frankfort
   to do some shopping, we needed some directions
         and nobody understood
         and nobody cared.
                  Do you know what I mean?
   You get this feeling
   of desperation
   and isolation
              and they're dumb and stupid—
                  so you talk LOUDER!
Have you ever noticed that when you talk
   to someone who doesn't speak English,
     you speak loudly and d-i-s-t-i-n-c-t-l-y!
       And you feel so frustrated
     because they still don't understand!
Can we lay down our *nationality*
            before the oneness of the Body?
Can we lay down our status—
       "neither bond nor free"?
   Can we lay down our sexuality—
      "neither male nor female"?
     God help us male chauvinists, every one!

How much Jesus cares about this.
  It is so important to Him that the
    dominant theme of His heart-cry
      on the night before He died
                    was that we affirm and
                  strengthen that oneness
                  that is ours
                in the shared life of Christ.
Don't let anything *separate* you in your fellowship of
  believers!
Don't let *anything* separate you in your church.
Now what was true in the church in Frankfort
    is true in the entire body of believers.
      What is it that separates you from
                        those around you?
                Whatever it is—it isn't enough!

Is it denominationalism?
      Some denominations are conservative.
      Some are liberal.
There are a lot of differences in the fellowship.
        But the differences are not enough to separate us!
Is it your life-style?
    Are you struggling to keep up with the Joneses?
      Are the Joneses struggling to keep up with you?
                *There is nothing that matters more
                          than our oneness.*

Look again at what Jesus said:
      Make them one *that the world may know.*
          If we want to make an impact on our world,
            those things that separate must bow down!
But we're masters at "splitting."
      And we know how to defend our stand
                      as a matter of principle
                  to preserve our integrity
                (meaning, "to protect our ego").

Jesus speaks to that:
>Don't let anything separate you!
>>Don't speak of compromise!
>>>Don't talk about maintaining principle
>>>>in the midst of division.

I think of our Lord, who,
>though he was in the form of God,
>did not count equality with God
>>a thing to be grasped,
>>but *emptied himself*
>taking the form of a servant,
>being born in the likeness of men.
>>(Philippians 2:6-7)
>>Jesus didn't lay aside what he *had*.
>>>He laid aside what he *was*.
>>>>*And that speaks to me!*

God's will is that we be one.
>And neither our language,
>>nor our culture,
>>>nor our race,
>>>>nor our heritage—
>>>>all the things that make us
>>>>what we are—*must separate us!*

We must ultimately bow at the foot of the cross,
so that our oneness in Christ may merge.
If the Holy Spirit of oneness would sweep
over individual communities of believers
until all the superficial barriers were broken down,
>and we would affirm each other
>>and live in our oneness in Christ,
>>the blessing and grace
>>and power of God could be present
in ways that we might never dream!
>>And the world would *know*—
>>And the world would *believe!*

Let us bow down now
    and place on the altar
            our nationality,
            our status,
            our sexuality,
            our prejudices,
              our all!
Let's bow before the Man at the head of the table—
                  and pass the bread!

Oh Jesus,

     who prayed that we might be one
      and died to make it so—
           we come to you.
  With all our prejudices we come.
        Our nationality is so important to us—
             our language,
               our sexuality,
                 our status.

  These things mean so much—
               and divide us so much!
          What needs to be done to make us one?

We thank you for our own church families.
I thank you for my own beloved denomination.
     But let us all know again that we belong to you—
          and we need each other.
     Don't let anything divide us! Don't let us
     defend our rights and preserve our integrity
        at the cost of the great integrity of the Body.
     This is hard for us, Lord—bring us to the cross
 and help us see how much it means to you—
       and give us grace to affirm it and live
         it like we really believed it.
      In your name and by your power,
              Amen.

Chapter Eleven
I VOTE YES ON YOU!
John 17:26)

Affirm is a neat word; "The wife"; The divine
Yes; "Please notice me"; When the vote is in.

Chapter 11

"Pass the bread" really means
to express our oneness by loving each other!
At the very close of the Prayer,
Jesus said something significant about love:
**I will make known [thy name], that
the love with which thou hast loved
me may be in them, and I in them.
(17:26)**

God is love.
Love is God.

I believe, too, that love is
our felt oneness behaviorized,
actualized in practice,
manifested in discernible acts of
Christlike caring.

Fundamentally, we *are* one.
But if I really *believe* it, I will *behave* it.

I will look at you.
  I will not judge you.
                If I really know that we are one,
                I will care for you as a person.
        I will affirm you.
Love is . . .
    caring for persons as persons,
        releasing persons,
            a steadfast refusal to judge.
                        In good, plain English
                    love means
                "I vote yes on you!"
Love means, on the basis of our oneness in Christ:
                I affirm you.

                            Affirm.
                    That's a neat word,
                            isn't it?

What it really means is:
        When the vote is in, I am on the affirmative side.
        I am *for* you.
        I vote yes on you as a person!
                        That doesn't mean
                        I like everything you do
                    or approve of the way you act.
                            Not at all.

Let me put it this way, because
sometimes, opposites help us to understand concepts.
We drive into the church parking lot.
        Just as we get there, another car parks nearby.
        We glance over to see who it is.   *Oh, no!*
We walk into the sanctuary, sit down,
        and there is that same person!   *Oh, no!*

We open up the bulletin:
>Sister So-and-So is singing today.   *Oh, no!*
>Pastor's sermon is on tithing.   *Oh, no!*

Meanwhile, back on the home front,
>the phone rings—pick it up—   *Oh, no!*
>the doorbell rings—open the door— *Oh, no!*

It is also possible for us to develop a "no" vote on
>those who are closest to us, isn't it?

I know some husbands who are forever saying No
>>to their wives.
>>>Every communication
>>is a put-down.
>>I am thinking of a guy
>who always refers to his wife
>as "The Wife,"
>>(but probably in lower case,
>>>"the wife.")
>And I feel like saying,
>"Hello, *The*, how are you?"
>>>Just No! No! No!

And there are wives who are always saying No
>>to their husbands.
>They can never do anything right.

Every story is interrupted seven times!
>"Honey, it wasn't Tuesday; it was Wednesday."
>"It wasn't nine o'clock; it was a quarter after."
>"It wasn't fifty dollars; it was five hundred!"
>"He didn't win it; he lost it!"
>>>You know,
>>he can never, ever
>>tell a story right!

Some children are always saying No to their parents.
>"You don't understand me."
>"You don't care."
>"Why can't you be like Marcia's parents?"

And some parents are always saying No to their
   children.
Maybe we think that saying No is the way to love them.
We are helping them to become better!
      "Will you ever be on time?"
      "Aren't you ever going to grow up?"
      "When will you . . ."
      "Why don't you . . ."
      When are you going to stop picking your
         pimples?"

                        I know that dates me.
                  My children can't stand the word
                              pimples,
                        and I hate *zits!*

Oh, we know how to say No all right!
My grandmother used to say that
            some people were just "cut on the bias!"
                  No!
                        No!
                              No!

Let's go back now and look at what
      a loving Yes can mean.
            I won't talk long about this.
            It is so beautiful that, if I do,
            you will begin to think you have died
                              and gone to heaven!
We are now in the parking lot of the church,
   and there "he" is, driving up nearby.   *Yes!*
We are sitting down in church
   and notice that Sister Smith is going to sing.   *Yes!*
The pastor gives the call to worship:
            I was glad when they said unto me,
            let us go into the house of the Lord.
                              Oh, yes!
   The room is messy.   *Yes.*
      The story is not quite right.   *OK.*

(Remember, it does not mean
that you approve of or agree with
everything.)
It doesn't mean that your heart is not broken
by the choices or life-styles of those you love.
It does mean that in your heart
you are saying:
I love you.
You are a person of infinite worth.
I say Yes to you because we are one.
Here's what I believe with all my heart:
In that Yes
the love of God is present!

Let's go back to Jesus' Prayer:
**. . . that the love with which thou
hast loved me may be in them, and
I in them. (17:26)**

Well, how did the Father love the Son?
The Father said Yes to His Son!
At His baptism:
Thou art my beloved Son:
with thee I am well pleased.
(Mark 1:11)

At His transfiguration:
This is my beloved Son;
listen to him. (Mark 9:7)

And, supremely, at the resurrection,
the Father was saying Yes to Jesus!

And Jesus said Yes to His Father:

My food is to do the will of him
who sent me, and to accomplish his work.
(John 4:34)
And the word which you hear is not mine
but the Father's who sent me.
(14:24)
I glorified thee on earth, having accomplished the work which thou gavest me to do.
(17:4)
My Father, if it be possible, let this cup
pass from me; nevertheless, not as I will,
but as thou wilt.
(Matthew 26:39)

The Father says Yes to the Son.
The Son says Yes to the Father,
and in the Son,
the Father says Yes to us!

There is a marvelous verse in II Corinthians 1:20:
For all the promises of God
find their Yes in him.
In Him, we have the guarantee of all His promises!
Right now, someone may be saying
No to you.
It may seem that the whole world is saying
No.
But God, In Jesus, is saying *Yes!*
He who did not spare his own Son but gave
him up for us all, will he not also give
us all things with him? (Romans 8:32)

God is saying Yes to us!
What I am thinking is that maybe we better
be passing it on—like passing the bread!

Here is where it all comes home:
    The Father's Yes
        and the Son's Yes,
            and the great Yes of the promises
                are to find their expression in our love
                    that says Yes to each other!

You know,
    it's an exciting thing,
        a scary thing,
            a wonderful thing
                to think about this!
    What if we really believed that God is saying Yes
                to us too
                    and that He won't quit!
        What if we really believed in each other
                        with a Yes love
                        that wouldn't quit!
    And what if we just didn't quit loving—no matter what!

What if someone makes a miserable blunder—
                and we just don't quit loving him?
What if somebody fails—
                and we keep right on loving him?
What if some insecure clown fouls everything up—
                and we love him anyway?
        What about the lonely ones,
                the insecure ones,
                    the unbeautiful ones?
    Could we, in the community of believers,
    warmed by the wonderful, undeserved
                            love of God—
        could we possibly just keep on loving them?
                    Oh, my goodness!
                If there is any place like that
                        in this world,
                    I want to be there!

And I am hearing again the word of the Lord,
What are you going to do about loving?
You see, we have no alternative.
There are no options.
Love is commanded.
Therefore, our response must be
in the actualizing of our oneness.
As we create a
non-judging,
affirming,
loving atmosphere,
what life-changing miracles can happen!
What beautiful transformations will take place
when we stop saying No
and start reflecting the Yes of God in Jesus.
Well, are you ready to vote?
All in favor, say *Yes!*

Father,
Can we really believe that you say Yes to us?
We know it in our heads.
Help us believe it in our hearts.
Lord, who am I saying No to?
Give me the vision to see others in the
light of your love for me,
and the grace to say Yes!
We thank you for your loving, affirming Yes.
And we respond in thanks and praise
with our own Amen!
Yes!

Chapter Twelve

WHO ME, LORD?

(In review)

I am a disciple; "The eschatalogical manifestation"; In times like these; On hearing and doing the words of Jesus.

Chapter 12

Well, I want us to go back one more time
and run this Priestly Prayer though our small
computer,
and push the button labeled "they."
I find myself increasingly concerned about
these "they" verses in which Jesus talks
about disciples.

Who me, Lord?
Are you talking to me?
I think so!

By the grace of God—I am a disciple!
Are *you?*
Well, *are you?*
If you are, nod your heads a little bit.
The Lord may be looking on and would like to know.

I'm not saying by that that we are making any
rash statements about ourselves.
But I believe that, despite our needs and
our weaknesses,

by the grace of God
WE ARE DISCIPLES!
And I think that what
Jesus says *about* us, *to* us, is important *for* us.

Let's gather up some of these "they" passages:
They have kept thy word.
(John 17:6)
Now *they* know that everything
that thou hast given me is from thee;
for I have given them the words which
thou gavest me,
and *they* have received them
and know in truth that I came from thee;
and *they* have believed that
thou didst send me.
(v. 7)
***They* are thine. (v. 9)**
***They* are in the world. (v. 11)**
And in case you didn't hear it:
***They* are not of the world.**
(v. 16)
If I were to attempt to characterize disciples,
I don't know what I would write down!
But Jesus, in these simple statements recorded by John,
described His disciples—
all of us!
When I summarize these verses,
I come up with four basic statements,
four things Jesus said about us; really,
two pairs of things:
One and Two: Disciples keep Jesus' words;
therefore
they know who Jesus is.
Three and Four: They are in the world;
but
they belong to God.

We've talked about some of these things in
earlier chapters.
Now let's put them all together!
Taking it from the top,
Jesus said that disciples keep His words;
therefore, they know who Jesus is.
When I was in the process of working through John 17
and trying to learn it
and read it
and outline it
and memorize it
and get it into a thinkable,
talkable form,
I started working through these "they" sections.

I made a list and I started
at the top
just as naturally and instinctively
as anything in the world.
*Disciples know who Jesus is; therefore, they keep His
words.*
I wrote that down just as
nicely as could be.

Then I went on to the other verses.
But I kept going back to those first verses
and thinking about them, and I read the prayer
again,
and do you know what I discovered?
I found that my natural, instinctive
order of things was *totally reversed!*
I had written: *Disciples know; therefore, they obey.*
But that order is precisely reversed
in this prayer
and in the New Testament itself.
Disciples obey; therefore, they know!

Do you know what we are prone to do?
   We try too often to convince people who Jesus *is*,
                              what He has done,
                              what He stands for,
and we come on in a teaching,
                     doctrinal,
                        defensive,
                           or sometimes,
                              unfortunately,
                                 offensive way.
                              When I began to see
                           what the order really is,
                        it was such a relief! Because
                     if you have to convince people
                  who Jesus is before you can get
                  them to obey, you've got to be a
               lot smarter than the people you talk to!

As wise as we are,
      that does somewhat limit the field, doesn't it?
      And it's a marvelous thing just to relax
         in the understanding that we do not have to have
                              all the answers!
      Our task is not to meet the objections and
                        questions of all comers,
but to begin at the point of obedience
   and not at the point of full understanding.
                     So the thing that's been so
                  great in my own life is simply
                  to understand that I do not have
                  to begin with the assurance of who
                  Jesus is and then come to obedience;
            rather, if I will obey, I will come to understand!
There is absolutely no way to communicate to you
   the depth of the revelation
                     that that concept has brought about
                              in my life!

Listen again to Jesus:

I have given them the words which thou gavest me,
and they have received them and know in truth that
I came from thee; and they have *believed* **that thou**
didst send me. (John 17:8)

The point of beginning is the point of obedience!

I really do believe that!

Do you suppose that,
when those first people met Jesus,
they knew all about Him?

When Jesus first encountered
the men who later followed Him,
I don't believe they knew who He was completely.
I think they knew a little bit.
They had been together in an intimate fellowship,
but they did not understand all about Jesus.
They didn't know about

the shepherds,
the star,
the manger,
the angel.

They didn't know about those things.
They didn't know about "the other wise man."
They hadn't heard about the littlest angel.
They knew nothing about the little drummer boy.
No awareness of "Amahl and The Night
Visitors."

I marvel that they could get saved at all!

Lovers of myth we are.
The first followers didn't know all these things,
but
they began to follow
and listen
and hear!

Through days and weeks and months,
they began to say Yes!

I love this line:

**I have given them the words which thou gavest me,
and they have *received* them.**

> *Received.*
> Isn't that a beautiful word?
> They have *received* them.
> They have *let them in.*
> They have *come to know!*

Then one day Jesus took the disciples up north
  to Caesarea Philippi
    and said to them:

**Who do you say that I am?
(Matthew 16:15)**

Peter answered first, of course:

> You are the Christ,
> the Son of the living God.
> (v. 16)

And Jesus said:

**Blessed are you, Simon, Bar-Jona!
For flesh and blood has not revealed this
  to you, but my Father who is in heaven.
(v. 17)**

Here is a revelation of God
that did not come
at the beginning,

> *but in the middle.*

It came as a result of days and weeks and months of
> following,
> responding,
> obeying,
> listening,
> hearing,

> and, gradually, there was that
beautiful dawning when the Holy Spirit opened up to
  them

> *who Jesus really was!*

I believe it's the same for us.
            Someone typed this out on a card for me
                        and left it on my desk:
Jesus said to them, "Who do you say that I am?"
And they said, "You are the eschatological
manifestation of the ground of our being.
You are the *kerygma,* magnified in conflict
and decision in the humanizing process."
                                And Jesus said,
                                    "What!!"
                            "You are Messiah!"

Assurance does not begin with our relationship with
    Christ.
    It is really the growing bottom line to our obedience.
Wherever you are on your journey,
    if there is doubt and confusion and
        misunderstanding,
            and you're trying to figure out
                        what's what,
                        who's who,
                        what's the gospel all about,
                        what's dumb,
                        what really matters,
                        what's cultural,
                        what's right,
                            who is Jesus,
                            what's He all about,
                I think there is a word of the Lord for us.

As we begin to obey, we will come to
growing assurance and certainty!
I believe that with all my heart!
            We want some experience to lift us up
                like the tide and set us down
                        in a world of confident assurance!

We want a gospel *experience* that brings us
the emotion and joy
that eliminate doubts and questions.
We want that.
May I repeat what I wrote earlier in the book?
It is *very* important to me these days
of my journey.
I'm learning that maybe
we don't need some great experience. We've
already had that. What we really need is
genuine,
careful,
deliberate
obedience to what we know!

So when I talk about obedience,
I'm not really talking about what we can't understand
and what we can't do.
I'm not talking about those words of Jesus
that are too much for us.
What bothers me are the words that are
understandable and *do-able!*
What is disturbing to me in my own life is
that it is so difficult to let the words of Jesus
come
down

into my daily conversations,
my daily patterns of thoughts
and response
and reaction.
Words like "Judge not."
Words like "Be not anxious."
Words that say, "You don't have to retaliate."
Words like "Take up your cross and follow me."
Words that tell me, "When you go to a banquet,
don't go wandering around the head table
looking for your name.

Just go in and sit down at the end somewhere.
If they want you, they'll come and get you."

Now the worst part of those words
that I have given to you from Jesus
is that I understand them.
I just understand them.
I don't understand all about them.
I have to have my own safety hatch,
but I understand them.
Don't you?

The marvelous thing about it is that
as we begin to obey,
in just the little things,
the little-big things,
our assurance grows,
our certainty grows.
Elton Trueblood said:
"The eyes of the soul are washed by obedience."
I think I believe that.

Now I'm not saying that all of our doubts and
all of our problems and all of our hassles
with the Christian faith
come from doubt and disobedience.
Just most of them.
It's just amazing how often underneath
the points of uncertainty and confusion and doubt
there is a closing of the eyes
or a turning away from
something
we know we really ought to do!
So much is solved by our simple, honest obedience
to Jesus!
That's a hard word, but a good word.
It's a word of judgment, but a word of hope.

I read about the young skeptic who loved to discourse
    with the guru who lived in a hut at the top of a
    mountain.
    The skeptic said: "Father, come out.
              I would talk with you
                    about my doubts."
    The old saint replied: "Son, come in.
              I would talk with you
                    about your sins."
         But that's a word of hope, isn't it?

I believe profoundly that when you begin to obey
        you begin to grow
                in security,
                in assurance,
                in confidence about who
                    Jesus is.
        What a privilege to know Jesus!

Do you know what Christian people say at a funeral
  or in a hospital?
They say, "I wonder what people do who don't know
  the Lord!"
            That's what we say to each other, isn't it?
My soul! What *do* people do without Jesus?
    I think about all the lonely people
            in the midst of the masses . . .
    I think about our industrialized,
                depersonalized,
                affluent,
                capitalistic society
      that has left deep,
                    black chasms and
              aching voids in the hearts of people.
I think about those people trying to
        fill those voids and those chasms
              with so many things that won't fit!

The occult,
commutes,
sex cults,
violence cults,
Satan worship,
   witches and warlocks!
            Can you believe
      that those are good, contemporary nouns?
I didn't even know what a "warlock" was
   until I watched "Bewitched" on TV!
      I never heard of this stuff. But it's here.
      It's a part of our culture and

                              it's scary!
                              It's awesome!

Then there is astrology.
Think of all the millions of dollars spent on that stuff!
                  I want you to know I don't
                        believe in all that.
         I'm a Scorpio and I'm skeptical!

During these times of our lives,
   these times of seething internal currents,
      these times of worldwide crisis and chaos—
                  we have a word!
That word is the teaching of Jesus
   supported by the affirmations of our faith.
      At the heart of our world—
      there is an anchor, a rock, a Savior!
      Do you know this song?
      In times like these you need a Savior,
      In times like these you need an anchor;
      Be very sure, be very sure,
      Your anchor holds and grips the Solid Rock.
                  RUTH CAYE JONES
            What a rock we have in Jesus!

And that beautiful knowledge of Him does not
                              belong exclusively
                                to the few who happen
                                to have the right personality
                                or the right "genes and corduroys"
                                or have had a fantastic experience!

Of course, I thank God for those who have had
                              "fantastic" experiences.
I talked with a guy at school one time who
          had been wallowing around in a life of sin.
He had wandered and searched—trying to find
                                            himself.
                    He had a mother who prayed for him.
                        And he said he had a vision that Jesus
                        came to where he was and talked to him.
                    He tried to talk himself out of what he had seen,
                              but the vision wouldn't go away.
                              It was a radical, transforming vision
                                        and it was real.
That's great, but
I don't know what that is.
I never did see anything like that.
I've got no data to handle a thing like that.
                                It doesn't compute.
Most of us come to this beautiful knowledge of Jesus,
          not by some out-of-this-world experience,
                        but by *simple, honest obedience.*
I'm thinking of Judas, not Iscariot, who asked:
    "Lord, how will you manifest yourself to us, and
                              not to the world?"
Jesus said:
    If a man loves me, he will *keep my word,*
        and my Father will love him,
    and we will come to him and make our home.
                        Isn't that beautiful?
                        Just like that!

I'm thinking of a story that I've heard all my life.
   Jesus told it at the end of the Sermon on the Mount.
   A wise man . . . built his house upon the rock
                              Remember that story?
   and the rain fell, and the floods came,
   and the winds blew and beat upon that house,
                   but it did not fall
     because it had been founded on the rock.
   And every one who hears these words of mine
   and does not do them will be like a foolish man
   who built his house upon the sand;
   and the rain fell, and the floods came,
   and beat against that house, and it fell;
                 and great was the fall of it.
                 (Matthew 7:24-27)

I've heard those words all of my life and,
   after all these years, *I'm beginning to hear them!*
In times like these,
                    we need an anchor!
   The song warns: *Be very sure, be very sure,*
                   Your anchor holds and grips
                              the Solid Rock!
Well, how do you build on a rock?
How do you know that your life has been made secure?
What is the key to that stability that can outlast
                    the rain,
                    the winds,
                    the floods?
                Hearing and doing the words of Jesus.
                           Just like that!
I don't know about you,
   but this whole thing meets me right where I am,
      with my needs,
         my struggles,
            my desires
               for the rest of my life!

I care what happens to me
the rest of my life.
It isn't going to be that long!
I have no desire to die on the vine.
I don't want to go Blah! until I die.
I really do care what happens to me
in the next twenty years.
Do you?
Yes, you do!

Where is newness for *me?*
Shall I wait around for some holy zap?
Where are *you?*
Are you waiting for Jesus to come to the foot
of the bed?
What will be the source of certainty in our lives?
What will be the base for understanding,
insight,
growth?
I think I know. It's the same for me as for thee.
As you and I listen to, and respond to, and obey
THE WORDS OF JESUS
my life will be builded on the rock,
and so will yours.
Are you listening?
Am I listening?
Jesus has some words for us!

Oh Jesus,

Your words are so near to us—so available.
Can it be that we are not really listening?
Are we looking everywhere else—listening
to everything else?
Quiet us to hear you—
open our hearts to your life-giving words.
They are beautiful,
wonderful words of life
and we really do need to listen.
Amen.